Windows to Heaven

Footprints of Faith and the Grace of God

By

Richard D. Brown

Copyright © 2010 by Richard D. Brown

Windows to Heaven
by Richard D. Brown

Printed in the United States of America

ISBN 9781609574550

All rights reserved solely by the author. The author guarantees all contents are original and do not infringe upon the legal rights of any other person or work. No part of this book may be reproduced in any form without the permission of the author. The views expressed in this book are not necessarily those of the publisher.

Unless otherwise indicated, Bible quotations are taken from The King James version of the Bible. Copyright © 1976 by Thomas Nelson, Inc. Nashville, Tennessee.

www.xulonpress.com

To: Nina,

Now, my friend forever.

Love, Richard D. Brown
(NICK BROWN)
NICKB@EROLS.COM
Dec. 4, 2019

Acknowledgements

I wish to thank my wife Peg and family for encouraging me to commit my stories to written form. Heartfelt recognition is given to my stepdaughter Rini Segar, Rini Jean Photography, for use of the cover pictures. I wish to thank God for inspiration and revelation.

Table of Contents

Preface xi
Early Memories 15
Talking to God at Twelve Years Old 18
A Bear Cave: Where Fools Dare to Trod 22
Remembering Bessie Smith 32
If There is a Devil, There Must be a God 37
Flat Rock River 42
Saving a Drowning Scout 46
Track – Lessons for Life 49
Life Altering 52
The Little Pig Was a Devil 56
Fighting Fires in California 61
Seeing the Pope 65
Evil Soldier Lurks 68

A Fire Tower—Where Fools Dare to Step............71
Brutal Attack Over TV 76
Diatoms Under Water...81
Students on Earth Day 90
Student Crossing the Room 94
Angel in the Woods..98
Mayor in Malaysia 106
Aborigine 112
Deadly Oil Palms 117
Bay of Bengal 120
Elephants in Sri Lanka 125
Gas Transportation Plan..129
Near Death Experience 137
My Will 144
Ian's Interactions with the Spiritual World 148
Here By the Grace of God 160
Palms On the Table 171
Passing It On..175
Alligator Attack..189
A Daughter is Drowning 197
Church on the Prairie 201

Neighbors Can Be Everlasting Friends	204
Singing	209
Traveling	213
The Great Adventure	223
Afterthoughts	257
Epilogue	263

Preface

Why would I write a book like this? I certainly am not a saint. I guess we all are sinners and sometimes saints. I'm not seeking acclaim or notoriety. And, probably many have seen God at work in his or her life. Many have even talked to Him. So, how is this book different?

I have not seen or heard of many books that document an individual's direct interaction with God or Jesus. There are many stories, such as some of these, of near death experiences and of miracles. But, ask anyone if they have personally talked to God and He actually talked back. If they say yes, the response often is "call the loony bin."

As I pass seventy years in age, I have decided to document stories of God's direct intervention in my life and in the lives of those around me. Other stories deal with people living spiritual lives. In doing this, I can testify that God is real and is with us on a daily basis. Maybe these stories will motivate others to reflect on their own lives and to document their blessed moments with God. Often, we become so busy in life that we fail to stop and accept that God has been more with us than not.

For me, my journey through life has not been noteworthy from a religious or pious point of view. At times, I placed priority upon material and intellectual rather than spiritual things. I have been caught up in the hustle and bustle of Washington, DC, being self-centered. From time to time, I have not been kind to my rivals. Some times, I have not been considerate to those sharing the same highway.

I guess I'm just an average guy trying to make a go of it in the human race. I was told in my early catechism classes that our purpose on earth is to know, love, and serve God. We are to strive to be spiritual beings, like Christ. In time, I have realized that perhaps we are spiritual beings learning to be human. Sometimes a doorway between heaven and earth opens and we find ourselves face to face with truth, eternity, and pure love. At that moment we are astonished, speechless, and in wonderment. For a short time, its as if our heart stops beating and reality, as we know it takes on a whole different meaning.

I have been blessed now and then to see through that open doorway and to view God's handiwork. At times, I was oblivious of the momentous event until it was over. Occasionally, I was conscious and awestruck as the experiences unfolded before me.

Some stories reflect "Nick", the child, young adult, husband, father, and grandfather of my Gemini personality. Others reflect the persona of "Dr. Brown". Seldom do both characters appear at the same time. Can you tell the difference?

I also included some person-to-person remembrances that are rather poignant. The names of my close friends and Grandchildren have been changed to protect their identities.

Some memories reflect tear-jerking thoughts or observations born out of solitude. For clarity, I have included some words in the form of prose penned at the time of a particular event.

Come with me on my journey. Can you reflect on yours?

Early Memories

My earliest memories of God center on God being kind, yet omnipotent. These conceptions emerged from my Roman Catholic upbringing, catechism classes, and parochial education. Existing essentially as an only child, my brother being eleven years older, I often found myself talking to God as my friend. I don't know why I developed a personal relationship with God, because I also knew He was all-powerful and to be feared.

When I was nine years old, I began to write things down. These were random thoughts, notions, and poems. My family lived in Elmwood Park, Chicago, when I wrote this poem as a bedtime prayer to God:

Dear God, Creator above,
>   let me offer my love.
For, it could be much worse,
>   let me put it in a verse.

Bless my mother tonight,
>   she is pretty and very bright.
She can cook, and bake, and sew,
>   and love.

Bless my father too
>   and all his things.
For, he gave us this house, this lot,
>   this everything.

Bless my brother
>   in a far away town.
Bless my relatives,
>   all around.

Bless this earth,
>on which we stand.
For without it,
>there would be no land.

Bless the universe
>too,
And, most important,
>You.

(Thoughts before sleep, 1947)

Looking back, it is interesting to note that, even living in an urban environment, I felt an empathy with the earth and its land. This feeling would become nurtured and fruitful as I matured.

Talking to God at Twelve Years Old

Was I naïve? Did I know from which I spoke? I probably was not the most deliberate person when, at 12, I spoke to God concerning universal questions and a proposed mutual contract.

It happened on our family farm in rural Indiana. We moved to the farm when I was eleven, after my father retired from Commonwealth Edison electric company in Chicago. The farm had been in my mother's family for many years, originating from a land grant as part of the Northwest Territory.

It was fun to roam the farm and I quickly developed a bond with the land. I developed a sense of wonder and respect for the natural world. I formed a kinship, not only with plants and animals, but also with the soil and rocks, including fossils of an earlier world. I felt close to historic Indians and their collected artifacts, to the wandering gypsies, and to my relatives and neighbors who worked the land. I felt a part of nature and wanted to protect it. I learned intimately what sod waterways, contour farming, and terracing could do to conserve and protect the land. This was the beginning of my calling, to be a natural scientist.

The farm was only 40 acres, just right for retirement. The farm produced soybeans, corn, and wheat, with an occasional crop of mixed clover and alfalfa. My father shared profits with those who actually cultivated the land. We took care of a garden, chickens, and the barn lot.

Near the garden was a grove of old walnut trees, which served as my sanctuary. Within it, I built a small shed with some old boards. The tall trees that bent over my little abode seemed to create a safe haven from having to face the ordeals and troubles of oncoming adulthood. At night, the canopy of stars gave the impression that my little dwelling was a portal to the universe. Consequently, I began to contemplate God as the all-powerful creator.

For a young farm boy without any siblings, God can become a very personal friend. I thanked Him for my world of land and sky. I wanted to be an active part of His creation. So much was this desire that I decided to make a vow. I promised God that I would live my life according to His commands, if He would help me make a positive difference in His creation. I remember trembling as I made my pledge. Did I really dare to strike a deal with God?

I didn't realize that since birth I was to live my life for Him without any qualifications. Also, I didn't realize that I only had to ask anything of God in His name and He would respond. Later I would realize one just doesn't strike contracts with the Almighty.

As I look back over my life, I realize that of the "deal or no deal", God has kept His side of the bargain. He helped me get involved with conservation projects during high school. He helped me to get admitted into a good university program and to remain in school, even in light of my laissez faire attitude. He helped me to be noticed in graduate school and to be blessed with many fellowships. He helped me jump-start my professional career and He provided many opportunities for me to really make a positive difference in the world. God has done all of these things. Yet, I feel that I have let Him down in so many ways.

A Bear Cave: Where Fools Dare to Trod

This is a true story of how angels watch over you. Looking back, it is even hard for me to believe this happened to me; however, this is a true account. It is an account of how a pre-teenage boy can be very naive and foolish. I was that pre-teen. As such, it is a story passed on by my children and grandchildren as "bear cave story." The term itself sets the stage for this hair-raising narrative.

I love the environs of Sugar Creek, in west-central Indiana, just two miles from our farm. The stream drains southerly into the Wabash River, which feeds the Ohio River, which in turn feeds the Mississippi River. The area surrounding Sugar Creek contains many historic, pre-historic, and natural sites of interest. Even as a pre-teen, I loved roaming the outdoors, while checking out plants, animals, old Indian encampments, and so forth.

Many days, I would roam the banks of Sugar Creek, collecting fossils and quartz geodes, while examining Indian artifacts. I would wade in the stream to see aquatic insects and to fish. But the exploits of one particular day are deep-rooted within my mind.

I was enjoying one of my adventures, collecting pieces of crinoids from various riffles in the Creek. Crinoids were marine animals that lived in a large inland sea that once spread across Central Indiana. Tentacles of the organisms extended from the ends of long segmented stalks. The fossilized segments are known as "Indian Beads," since native Americans strung them into necklaces. Most of the fine specimens of crinoids in the Smithsonian Museum came from an embankment just upstream.

One day, while examining a large gravel bed in the Creek, I looked up the side of a high, honeycomb eroded sandstone cliff. The cliff face was about seventy-five feet high, rising steeply from the Creek bottom. About fifty feet above where I stood, there was a large-mouthed cave, which narrowed, reaching into the sandstone formation. Above the cave, a large overhang projected from the top of the precipice. Above the cliff, tall trees grew in a dense wooded terrain. Under the overhang, small scrub-like vegetation grew at the cave entrance.

The cliff face below the cave, comprised of barren and smooth sandstone, formed an insurmountable precipice. I tried many times to climb into the cave from the streambed. Each time, I would slide into the water after clambering only a few feet. The only way to reach the cave was to come down from the top. I *really* wanted to get into that cave.

The reality that a bear actually might be in the cave wasn't given a moment's thought. I was young, naive, and rambunctious— exploring was my nature.

Traits such as appearing foolish, irrational, and illogical were second nature. I went home to await a try at the cave the next day.

In the morning, I sneaked to the place beside our farmhouse where my mother sun-dried our newly washed clothes. I "borrowed" my mother's clotheslines. I found a solitary place where I tied the two long lengths of cotton rope together using overhand knots, about one foot apart. I was ready. With rope in hand, I rode my bicycle down the twisty road to the stream.

I hid my bicycle in some small bushes downstream from an old covered bridge that crossed Sugar Creek, near the cliff. I carried my rope in a circuitous route up through dense woods, exiting above the overhang. From the bottom, I had identified a particular tree that rose directly above the cave. I tied my rope onto the base of that tree, threw the rope over the cliff, and hoped for the best.

I lowered myself out over the edge of the ledge. I felt just like a mountain climber. A gentle wind blew across my face. I could see far downstream. Below me, I could see the flat rock bed of Sugar Creek. I thought that if I fell, that watery bedrock would be my demise. That only made it more exciting.

I lowered myself beyond the edge of the overhang. The knots held. Down I went, overhand by overhand. Do you know that when hanging on a rope lowered from an overhang that one tends to turn in a circle? I discovered that was so. How was I ever going to get into the cave, let alone be able to touch the rock face of the cliff? I was twisting in the breeze. I did not ponder my fate very long before the rope broke.

It seemed only an instant before I landed on a narrow ledge high on the cliff. Everything occurred so fast, I didn't have time to become frightened. I decided to stay where I landed for the rest of my life.

The ledge was about ten inches deep. I landed in a cramped position that quickly became uncomfortable. To my right, the ledge narrowed and disappeared into the cliff. To my left, the ledge extended to the mouth of the cave. The only way out of my predicament was to use the ledge to enter the cavernous opening.

Stranded on a narrow ledge on the side of a cliff can be daunting. More terrifying is the process of rising to a standing position on such a prominence. Slowly, I stood. (Spiderman would be proud of me!) Leaning against the cliff, I sidestepped toward the cave.

I did it! I reached the vegetation at the gaping entrance of the grotto. I held on for dear life. Grasping roots, I pulled myself into the cave. The rear of the cave was indefinite. I could not tell how deep the cave went into the sandstone formation. Darkness hid identification of any rock, plant, or animal features. Should I venture further?

My question was soon answered. Within seconds, I heard a loud rustling noise coming from within the cave. What could be making such a loud sound from this remote refuge, a so-called "Bear Cave"? My choices were limited. I did the only thing that came to mind. I left the Bear Cave.

I looked toward the ledge where I fell. There was nowhere to go. On the other side, a somewhat wider ledge extended to the edge of the cliff. This was the way to go. Without looking back, I scurried onto the ledge, again doing my side step. Quickly, I eased myself to the end of that ledge. And, that was the end. Stuck high on a cliff, probably being chased by a bear, I executed the only option to a kid. I jumped.

After all, superheroes on television jump off high structures such as buildings, towers, and cliffs, and survive just fine. Once, I saw a hero jump into thin air to grab tree limbs that lowered him to safety. I could do that.

As I jumped, I spread my arms very wide, thrusting myself from the cliff toward some mature trees located by the side of the cliff. As an aside, when one does this, acceleration occurs incredibly fast. A high wind speed causes one's eyes to blur as they fill with tears. Perhaps this was not an issue for superheroes but it was for me.

I was good and my timing was just right. My arms closed just as I entered the small limbs of a treetop. If I could gather enough limbs and hold on, they would slow my velocity and lower me to the ground. Sure enough, it worked!

I held on and felt myself slowing down. Though my heart was throbbing, I was going to be saved, or so I thought. Instead of lowering me neatly to the ground, the limbs swung me down in the direction of the tree trunk! I remember thinking, "This is going to hurt!"

Do you know what? It hurt. I slammed into the trunk of a tall, young oak tree. As I hit the tree, I clung for all I was worth. My grip did not hold as I slid down that tree trunk. "Ouch!" was all I thought, in a repeated loop. Soon, I saw the forest floor. I let go and fell into the soft leaf litter. I was safe. I was alive. I'll never do it again, I promised.

I was hurt and was bleeding from the many cuts and abrasions sustained as I slid down the trunk like a petrified fireman. Alone, I could not hope for help. I limped back to my bike, holding my chest and sides, somehow thinking that act would make them feel better. In great pain and with great difficulty, I peddled my bicycle the long two miles home. As I rode up to the house, I fell off of my bike and staggered the last few yards—where my mother was waiting. I was hoping for some motherly sympathy, but instead, mother looked at me and said just one thing, "Where is my rope?"

I think my mother thought I had it coming. I had to take care of my wounds. Luckily they were superficial. It took about two weeks for the cuts and bruises to disappear. I had to buy my mother new rope. Over the next two years, whenever I visited Sugar Creek, I still could see that broken rope dangling from the overhang. I was glad when it finally disappeared.

Looking back, I try not to dwell on lessons learned. I do wonder why I tried such a ridiculous stunt in the first place. Why didn't a twelve year old boy have any sense? Why did I use that old rotten cotton rope? Why didn't I think that I might dangle in thin air after lowering myself from an overhang? What was my plan should I find a bear? How was I going to get down from the cave? How, what, and why, indeed!

There is one enduring lesson that has remained with me throughout my life. Wherever I travel, I always carry rope. I mean good synthetic, high-strength rope, and plenty of it. It is in the trunk of my car and behind the seat of my pickup truck. It was also in the trunks of vehicles of the teenage girls that I raised. And yes, there have been impetuous adventures in my adult life where I have needed the rope. Some of those stories will be told later.

Remembering Bessie Smith

Her name was Bessie Smith. She lived with her mother about two miles from my childhood farm. She was in her late seventies and her mother was close to one hundred years old. Both were weathered by years of sun exposure. They lived on a farm at the corner of a county boundary road and the start of a county road leading toward my farm. Both roads were dusty from decades of the grading of their gravel ridges and pot holes.

Bessie and her mother lived in an old wood clapboard-sided farm house fronting the county road. Its white paint was faded and pitted from sand particles strewn from the road. It was a simple house with a front room, a kitchen, and two rear bedrooms.

Now, why would two twelve year old boys ride their bicycles over two miles of gravel roads to visit Bessie and her mother? Need one even ask an explorer? I can say that our visits over a four year period were an excursion into another world. My best friend Dean and I found welcome, comfort, security, and transport into a world lost in history during our visits.

Our first encounter with Bessie and her mother was during a bicycle ride in the summer of 1950. In rural Indiana, a bicycle ride is a combination of exploration and wonder as our bicycles would slip and slide through the gravel, often skirting snakes, land turtles, and rabbits. As we approached the county line intersection, we saw Bessie and her mother in their vegetable garden hoeing weeds. We waved and stopped to say hello. They were gracious and very thankful for two boys taking an interest in their cherished garden. Few people stopped to visit, so we were a pleasant surprise.

Bessie showed us her favorite gooseberry plants, explaining that "gooseberries make excellent pies, as long as you use lots of sugar." The long rows contained carrots, lettuce, tomatoes, potatoes, and lots of green beans. Along the sides of the garden were cucumbers, watermelons, squash, and pumpkins.

Beside the vegetable garden was a flower garden, even larger in size. Bessie told us the names: coneflowers, peonies, nasturtiums, hollyhocks, irises, asters, and many others. Bessie and her mother would be in the gardens at dawn, working until noon. Then, they would rest during the heat of the day until evening. During our first and many following visits, Bessie would invite us into her home for some iced tea with fresh spearmint.

One day, Bessie mentioned that she had a Ford Model A in the barn. We chomped at the bit to see it. She walked us to the barn where the Model A stood covered under loose straw and nesting pigeons. We begged her to take us for a ride. She said that she would clean it up and take us for a ride the next time we came down. About a week later, we rode down to see her and she kept her word. I even got to drive it (sort of). She let me steer, while I "retarded the spark" and operated the throttle. It puttered similar to a gas-operated lawn mower in tall grass. I was surprised to find the Model A skidded along the gravel roads just like our bikes.

On many visits, we would just sit and talk. Bessie would ask us about the things we did at school and things of interest to us. When I mentioned I was interested in track, she said, "Why don't you run down here?" The next time I went to visit her, I did.

Now, almost 60 years later, I still clearly remember those days with Bessie Smith and her mother. They would reach out and befriend any visitor. Bessie was a model of how to place others before one's self.

Bessie and her mother seemed to have the "good life", peaceful with God and love of neighbor. Although not in church, I think those days were our first exposure to godliness. I think we learned a lot from Bessie. I think we learned moral and mature character. We need more Bessie Smiths.

If There is a Devil, There Must be a God

What does a fourteen year old boy do during winter on a small rural farm? Why, he moves small objects with mental powers. "Of course you did," you say. Well, I say "I did!" Looking back, I think that I agree that adolescent kids have excessive energy available to them. I have heard of teenagers turning radios, TVs, lamps, and the like on and off, just by walking in and out of a room. I don't remember affecting electronic devices, but I have witnessed some very weird special effects.

I don't know why I started to practice moving small objects; probably because life can be very boring for a single boy in a rural farmhouse. I think that I noticed slight movement of nearby pieces of paper when I looked at them. Yes, I saw illusionists and magicians move objects on TV. Perhaps, I thought I could do the same. In time, I could move post cards, pencils, and paper clips. Their positions would never change by more than an inch, but movement is movement. I thought that I was on top of the world. I could be famous.

Hanging from the ceiling of my bedroom was a large four-tier mobile. My older brother had made it from colored cardboard and coat hangers. The bottom tier was almost four feet across. The entire mobile hung about two feet from the ceiling. Each tier hung independently from the others.

After dark, I would spend evenings in my room listening to a short wave radio as I lay in my bed staring at the ceiling and trying to move the mobile. I would cover up all air vents and door cracks to make sure air currents did not affect the mobile. At first, it would not move and I decided that moving objects using the mind was a lot of bunk. I was surprised one night when I thought I detected a slight movement.

After about two months of practice, I could move the mobile at will. I could move one tier one way and another tier another way. I even could move all of the tiers in the same direction. To assure myself that I was, in fact, moving the mobile, I would turn all of the tiers around in one direction until I could sense a slight resistance as the suspension string became taut. Upon release, the mobile would slowly unwind. When it would begin to unwind, I would mentally stop its movement and continue to turn the mobile in the original direction.

"Wow!" was I good or what? Cockiness is a sure fire path to disaster. I was proud that I had conquered the forces of nature. I knew little of the forces that really lay in wait.

This is the point that my story becomes scary. One night, when pushing the mobile around in one direction, I felt a slight resistance as it stopped. I pushed harder. As it began to move again, I felt a stronger resistance. The resistance affected the entire mobile, in a sense resisting everything I would try to do. I pushed harder, as hard as I could. This was a mistake.

I felt a strong unseen presence in the room and a sensation of dread. My attempt at moving the mobile was met with a force that was very strong, and frightful. All of a sudden, the mobile spun backwards as fast as a fan blade. I was terrified. Had I summoned up an evil spirit? Was I doomed? What did I unleash? I felt an evil presence in the room. Did I invoke the devil? Was this my punishment for toying with occult activity?

The mobile continued to spin. No air currents were present, except for those created by the mobile itself. I shrunk back, pulling the bed covers over me. An impending sense of doom filled the room. I had been challenged by a very powerful force and lost the match hands down.

I asked God for help. I asked in the name of Jesus that the evil presence leave forever. Abruptly, a peaceful calm came about as the mobile became motionless. Then and there, I promised myself and God that I would never again try to move objects.

Have I ever wondered if I can still move objects? Yes, I have. I am content to leave it at that. Wouldn't you?

Flat Rock River

This is another story of loss of life averted. First, it should not have happened. Second, total survival should not have occurred. God must have been watching over all of us when this happened.

When I was twenty-one, I took a group of boy scouts on an overnight campout. The campsite was on an island in the Flat Rock River in east central Indiana. The purpose of the trip was to allow the group to fulfill requirements for a pioneering merit badge.

It was a sunny day and we looked forward to having a good time. The river was low, making it easy to bring supplies by canoe to the small island.

The island had no amenities. We were going to "rough it."

It was nearing dark by the time that we had our tents raised, fires built, and meals started. I noticed that the river was rising. I thought, "It's not raining. There's nothing to worry about." Unbeknownst to us, a severe storm had drenched the upstream watershed. Soon, the water was in the camp and getting deeper and deeper. Tents had to be moved. It was clear that something unusual was happening and I began to worry.

Water was rising all around. We converged at the center of the island, along with snakes, large spiders, and other critters. We packed up, not needing to douse our fires. It was time to abandon the island. Normally this would not be a problem, but now it was pitch black night and beginning to rain. River currents suddenly became treacherous. Salvation, however, was a sure bet, because we had good flashlights and I had plenty of trusty rope.

At the downstream end of the island, I tied one end of rope to the front end of one of the canoes and set it adrift with two of my most trusted scouts. They were to use their paddles to swerve the canoe to the far shore, similar to the swing of a pendulum, as I held onto the other end of the rope.

It worked! Now, they were to walk their end of the rope upstream to a point parallel to the upstream end of the island. We now had a strong safety line. Using this rope, we were easily able to ferry the entire group onto the far shore using our canoes. I was in the last canoe. As I detached my rope from the island and swung downstream toward the shore, the island disappeared under water.

That night, we camped on the shore of Flat Rock River. Slightly wet and a little worse for wear, we survived. The next morning we packed and went home. Each boy scout had successfully earned his merit badge in pioneering.

Looking back, I wonder what we would have done without my trusty rope. My childhood experience at the Bear Cave with rotten cotton rope proved to be a vital lesson learned. Our Great Scoutmaster had watched over us.

Saving a Drowning Scout

I guess I can admit this now. When I was a boy scout, I could not swim. In rural Indiana in the early 1950s, one had to travel many miles to a swimming pool. As scouts, we would travel fifty miles to a YMCA. Although swimming tests were administered, we went there for fun, not for swim lessons or tests.

My rural friends learned very young to dog paddle in swimming holes, an opportunity not available to me during my early upbringing in Chicago. Since knowing how to swim is requisite for an Eagle rank, it goes without saying that I did not attain that elite level. However, I did achieve a record for merit badges (fifty).

Upon leaving active Marine Corps duty at twenty years old, I became an assistant Scoutmaster. It was the summer of 1958 when I took a small group of scouts to a local swimming hole in Sugar Creek. The swimming spot was located under a short covered bridge where the Creek flowed within a narrow gorge. A steep rock face was on both sides of the stream.

The swift whirling current created a deep hole in the middle of the gorge, bounded by chest-high water suitable for swimming. Nevertheless, the sheer walls of the gorge prohibited easy escape. To think I led young boys into perilous waters is unsettling. That I thought they all could swim was even more unsettling, even to this day.

It was a hot day, making the cool water a welcome relief. The whole escapade was fun and turning out to be a success until a scout came to me, saying another scout was drowning. He had slipped into the deep hole!

I could not swim. What was I to do?

I jumped into the water upstream and floated toward the hole. I could not see the scout. He was under the water, unable to keep afloat. I dove under the water. Since I sink without difficulty, I was able to get to the bottom of the cavity, place my hands under the boy and push him to the surface. I walked on the bottom until we were out of the deep water.

The scout gasped for air as I led him downstream to an exposed pile of gravel rocks. The group yelled, "Hooray!" proclaiming me a hero. Not wanting to enrage their parents, I downplayed the incident. Of course, I wouldn't have blamed the parents, having taken their sons into dangerous water without the means to save them!

Thank God that I could hold my breath. My years of track activities and Marine Corps life had enlarged and strengthened my lungs to the point that I could hold my breath under water for a very long time. Since that time, I learned how to tread water and do a modified breaststroke.

Track – Lessons for Life

In high school, I ran and lettered in track. It was what I could do. I wasn't coordinated enough for basketball, where "traveling" and "double-dribbling" were my specialties. The rules of baseball always left me in a quandary as to when to run or not run. I always was tagged out or, worse, was responsible for getting one or more of my teammates tagged out.

Track was great. Except for relays, I did not have to worry about letting my team down. And fortunately, I was fast. I won most of my events and anchored relays. It was great and I was a star. While in the Marine Corps, and again when I was in graduate school, I was asked by official scouts to join an

Olympic Team. Initially, it was for the long jump but later on, for the mile run.

Yes, I thank God for track. It was my reality check and my claim to being the genuine article, the real deal. Running and jumping was my way of life in high school. I even built my own jumping pit on the farm! I would practice hours on end to hit the jump off board just at the right time and place in order to avoid "scratching." Scratching is jumping from a place beyond the jump off board causing one to be disqualified. Jumping into the air for 25 feet or more felt like flying.

When I was young, I would run rather than walk. While in the Marine Corp, I didn't mind running, even off base. One Sunday in San Diego, I ran quite a few city blocks in order to get to Catholic Mass on time. The police stopped me, leaving me in a tight situation, as I tried to explain why I was running. Later in my 40's I was stopped again, while running to quickly get though a dangerous neighborhood. Again, it was difficult to talk my way out of it.

Now, so many years later, it is difficult to find any trace of my running days. I've become overweight. I don't run or jog, but maybe I should. I do walk. Remembering my love of running and jumping came back to me this year when I went to my fifty-third high school class reunion. A man who had been a fellow student, though two years behind me, came up to me and said how he admired my running and worked hard to follow in my footsteps. He wanted me to know my running inspired him to excel at track events in high school and college. I thanked him and said to myself "I didn't know."

I guess I am left with pride in being a role model. I wonder if some other young man was inspired by my fellow alumnus. Does the saga continue?

Life Altering

Sometimes we find ourselves in a momentary incident that changes our lives. Often, we aren't even thinking about anything in particular when life change smacks us upside the head. It can seem unreal, almost spiritual. Such an event occurred when I was a junior in high school. It still brings tears when I think about it.

Yes, I stood out in track as a sophomore. But, as I elongated, became more muscular, and grew smarter upon entering my third year of high school, I really excelled. I would listen closely to the advice of my track coach. I also read a lot about the science of movement and ballistics of jumping. I read all I could about the life of Jessie Owens, a great Olympic track star.

My track coach was my uncle. He taught history as well as all of the male sports at the small school. He was well known for his integrity, truthfulness, and leadership skills. He was a wonderful family patriarch. He was one of my idols. His family nickname was "Pix."

One warm afternoon, he was working one-on-one with me to improve my long jumping distance. The sport was known at that time as "broad jumping." It required precise timing in order to jump off of a narrow board, without stepping over it. Then, one had to literally "walk in air" to achieve a great distance before landing in a pit containing sand or other soft material.

That day, Pix used his treasured yardstick to encourage me to attain a high arc before landing. He told me to jump beyond it before landing. He held it crosswise across the pit about six inches above the sand. It seemed that he held it far beyond the distance

I could attain. He was encouraging me to excel. For me, the assignment seemed impossible.

I took a long, fast run and hit the board at the right spot and sailed into the air. Since I was facing skyward, I could not see the yardstick. I hoped for my best. It wasn't good enough. I landed short of his goal and crashed onto the yardstick. It splintered loudly as I landed. The broken pieces flew far beyond the pit.

I felt so bad. I had broken his yardstick. It might seem trivial, but I knew it was treasured. He had long used it to point to places on his blackboard while teaching. It was a favorite teaching tool of his. Yes, other yardsticks were available. But, this one had history.

Pix could see that I felt awful. He knew my remorse and assured me it was okay. It may have been okay with him, but not for me. I had broken something close to him. I was so shaken that I could jump no more during that practice session. I just ran and ran around the track.

As life goes, it was not much of a catastrophe. I loved Pix. He was my role model. Accordingly, I held that moment as a principle that guided me for the rest of my life. From then on, in track and in life I would always try to excel just a little bit more.

Only recently, upon reflection, I realized that the principle became ingrained as a kernel of my being. I have not settled for less. I always would strive to do my best. The lesson became an essential part of all of my endeavors. I always tried to not break the yard stick. Pix never knew.

The Little Pig Was a Devil

In 1956, while in the Marine Corps, I spent a weekend with a comrade-in-arms rummaging through old silver mines. They were located in the Cimarron Mountains west of Tucson, Arizona. He knew the area well, this being his old teenage stomping ground. We rode out there from our base in San Diego in his old rattletrap of a sedan.

In those days, the locale seemed an endless, open desert with the sand broken by an occasional low lying cactus or tumbleweed. We drove across a broad expanse of desolate wilderness. The car seemed to lumber and it sputtered along as we gained elevation. Looking back, I could see a valley. We were going up an inclined plane, where the flat surface of the land was tilted. The grade was increasing as we went along.

After a half-hour, the rear wheels began to slip on the surprisingly steep slope. We stopped the car. We were finished riding. Ahead lay a sandy, inhospitable climb.

We reached the top of our ascent and began to look for openings of old mine shafts. In hindsight, I now realize how poorly the venture was conceived. The old mines had timbers riddled with dry rot, ready to cave in at any disturbance. And, the shaded grottos were havens for desert rattlesnakes. After seeing large spider webs at the openings of several shafts, I left my partner to fend for his own well being. I decided to wander around and look at the huge vistas. However, self assurance of my relative safety was unwise.

Behind me, I heard a low, guttural grunt. I looked around and saw nothing unusual. Looking again at the scenery, I heard a louder and more distinctive snarl. I looked back again. This time, I saw a small, pig-like animal looking at me and digging into the sand with its hoofs. It had a long tusk curving upward from each side of its mouth. Having only seen it in pictures, it undoubtedly was a Peccary, Desert Hog, a Javelina, or more precisely, a Collared Peccary. They are called Javelinas, (Spanish for "javelin" or "spear") because of their razor-sharp tusks.

Peccaries are known for being very ferocious when disturbed. Using their long protruding tusks, they can cause serious injury. I had seen signs which warned not to get too close because peccaries are aggressive and cannot be domesticated. What should I do?

I decided to back away. As I stepped backwards, the pig moved forward. I turned away, faced down slope, and walked forward. It followed, getting closer with each step. I decided to run.

Having been a track star, I thought that I easily could outrun a little pig. I started to jog down the mountain. It pursued. The chase was on. I began to increase my speed. The pig still was closing the gap. I was now running at full speed. Its grunts sounded louder.

I found myself bounding almost blindly over clumps of prickly cactus plants. Snakes, cacti, rocks, and who knows what, were in my path as I went vaulting down that long desert slope. After running about a mile, I looked back to see if my pursuer had vanished. It hadn't. It was only about thirty feet away, with head bent down and running fast. I continued to run at my fullest speed. This was going to be much more than a mile run.

My heart began to throb and my lungs began to sting. Could I ever outrun this beast? After running about two miles, I quit. The pig was a half mile behind me and standing still. I had run for my life and won.

Was the pig the devil incarnate? I doubt it. But, I sure prayed as I hurdled down in elevation. I think that God took pity on me that day.

The whole incident seems to have been a wake up call in complacency. Perhaps we take it for granted that life's serenity will be the same from one moment to the next. Since the battle with that little devil, I have become more aware of my surroundings.

I could see my companion's car far in the distance, near the top of the mountain. He spotted me, but had no idea why I ran. Eventually, he drove down to meet me. I knew he would.

Fighting Fires in California

I was nineteen years old and completing advanced training at Camp Pendleton in Southern California. I had completed a rough regimen of basic training and enjoyed a home furlough. I was feeling on top of the world, both mentally and physically. I was not in harm's way; or so I thought.

It never occurred to me that Southern California and wildfires were often used in the same sentence. It also by no means came to mind that Marine trainees would be called upon to fight such fires during emergencies.

It was around noon in early August when we were called to formation. We were told of a fire threat to the base, surrounding public lands, and homes. We would assist state and local firefighters by creating fire breaks and putting out lingering embers. It seemed fairly straight forward and I looked ahead to a departure from the rigorous training. We were assigned rations of food and water. Each was issued a fire retardant blanket and a collapsible shovel, attached to a backpack. Soon we were in trucks and headed to the fire lines.

When we arrived, we were taught how to put out smoldering fires, told about the importance of keeping hydrated, and shown how to use our fire retardant blankets. Then, we were led to a site at the side of a fire front where we would remove brush and dead vegetation, thereby creating a fire break.

We could hear the roaring fire. It blew through the sage brush that spread throughout the arid and hilly landscape. As the fire neared clumps of dry sage brush, the vegetation would explode like a flash bulb and sail into the air. Next, it would land a great distance downwind to start a new fire. I could not see how anyone could put out such a wildfire.

As we were digging trenches, we were given the bad news that the fire front had changed directions and headed right toward us. We gathered in a nearby clearing and dug shallow pits. We would get into these, cover with the fire retardant blankets, and wait until the fire had passed over our location.

I complied with the order without hesitation. I knew that the retardant blankets would reflect heat and provide a space for a firefighter to breathe. These protective devices were especially critical in such unpredictable wildfires.

One Marine in our unit declined to obey the order to wait out the oncoming firestorm. He claimed that he grew up in a similar environment and that he was a good runner. With that pronouncement, he took off running downhill, away from the fire. I could only say, "God speed!"

Soon, we were dug in, individually sheltered by our fire retardant blankets. We heard the intense roar of the fire as it passed over our clearing. I prayed for our safety, especially for those without the protection we had.

I did not feel especially hot or scared as the fire passed over. The fire blew over quickly and the "all clear" was announced. Upon emerging from my burrow, the utter devastation was evident in every direction. Only blackened earth and smoke-filled air greeted us. We were safe. We survived to fight the fire again.

The winds calmed and aerial tankers doused the fire front. We suppressed the remaining embers. Then we packed up and headed for home. It was just another day for Marines.

Back at our barracks, we were devastated when we were informed that the charred body of our comrade had been found, the one who had chosen to sprint from the fire. I was thankful for the disciplined training that had saved our lives that day. We missed our fallen comrade for a long time.

Seeing the Pope

During my brief, active Marine Corps career, 1956-1958, I was in a Special Forces unit. Although there are many stories I could recount, one stands out as it contains an evident interaction with The Almighty.

I was raised in the Roman Catholic Church. My father showed me the pious way of life. Veneration for church tradition, its Latin mass and its saints and images was held in high regard. As a result, a visit to Rome during a Mediterranean shore leave was a high point in my life.

I visited St. Peters, its basilica, and the Sistine chapel. I toured the catacombs and touched one of the feet of St. Peter's statue, a traditional gesture, and I touched the Pieta. I also went to the summer palace of the pope, in hopes of receiving a blessing.

When I arrived at Castle Gondalfo, its beauty took me aback. Butterflies and stunning flowers were everywhere. Crowds were assembling in the main plaza, awaiting the appearance of Pope Pius XII at one of the Castle's balconies.

It was over a decade since the end of the World War. The pope had been criticized negatively for not interceding on behalf of Europe's Jewish community during the Nazi occupation. Others lauded his efforts by being influential behind the scenes to save Jews. I did not know what to expect, Saint or fallen sinner. Bolstered by my faith, I was hoping to see a halo.

Suddenly shouts erupted all around, "Viva El Papa! Viva El Papa!" in a deafening cacophony. I looked high on the Castle wall and saw a small man on a small balcony. It was the Pope! I made the sign of the cross as he blessed the crowd.

Did he have a halo? I don't know. I did see something indistinguishable above his head. It was blurry. Could it have been a halo? Possibly, but it also could have been my own attempt to see what I wanted to see. Tears came to my eyes. I was seeing the Rock of the church, the direct descendent from the apostle Peter, the one who was infallible in matters of faith. It was a very moving moment. Was I seeing a living saint?

With the benefit of hindsight, I can only say, I saw a leading historical figure who led the Church during a pivotal period in world history. I feel that the world may never know what Pope Pius XII experienced, suffered, or achieved during the War. I choose to remember seeing a corona, however dim.

Evil Soldier Lurks

Evil is real. Thank goodness, it rarely manifests itself. I have come face to face with it on only a few occasions. Evil is one of those, "you know it when you see it," things. It is something you never wish to confront.

I saw evil in the Marine Corps in the form of a private in my squad. We arrived on a troop ship in Turkey to demonstrate recent improvements in battlefield communications. I was involved in showing new single sideband radio equipment. We remained on ship for a couple of days before moving by convoy into a rural area of the country.

The marine in question was a loner. He found fault with everything and hated authority figures. I wondered how he made it this far in the Corps. When I would talk to him, he would use bad language and blaspheme in every other sentence. He would look directly at me with seemingly bottomless dark eyes, filled with intense hate. I tried to have as little to do with him as possible.

One day, I asked him to perform some menial task. He moved close to me, peered into my eyes and said, "I'm going to kill you!" I responded, "For now, get your work done." Beyond doubt, I expected him to carry out his threat. I asked God to help me deal with the situation.

That night, I expected him to keep his word. In the middle of the night, I heard a slight noise, a swooshing of cloth against cloth, coming closer and closer to me. I was braced for the worst. Suddenly the private leaped on top of me in my bunk saying, "I've had enough of you," thrusting his bayonet to my stomach as he said it. At the same time, I thrust my bayonet hard against his stomach, surely breaking skin. I had concealed my bayonet beside me for such an assault. I then said, "If I go, you go!" He backed off and returned to his bunk.

The next morning, and thereafter, that private performed his duties as told, without griping in the least. I had dealt with him with the only language he understood, that of intimidation. Soon, he was transferred out of my unit. I did not hear of any problems with him after our confrontation.

Standing up for what you believe is right and sometimes takes a lot of courage. In this incident I relied on my Marine Corps backbone and trust in God. In retrospect, I think that I lived to tell this tale "by the grace of God."

I guess I knew that private was evil because I knew how to recognize evil. You know it by feeling its presence. It's a feeling you never forget.

A Fire Tower —
Where Fools Dare to Step

Some believe that the designations "youth" and "fool" are interchangeable. Looking back at my younger days, I can understand why. In fact, from the perspective of today, I can say, "What was I thinking?"

I was twenty-three years old and out of the Marine Corps. I had two sons, one and two years old, and a daughter only a few weeks old. I decided to take my wife and kids to a forest preserve and look out over the landscape from a fire tower. In the early 1960's, fire towers were rather simple structures without many safety features. You can see where I am headed with this.

I parked our car in a parking area fronting the tower. My wife stayed with the baby in the car. She had a clear view of the entire tower. I took the boys in hand and walked over to the tower. I waved goodbye to my wife.

The tower had high, open steps. The sides of the tower were open except for a handrail. It had five levels, including the top floor which was about fifty feet above the ground. I should have stopped at that point and turned back. But, youth has its priorities, such as saving face and stubbornness.

We started up the tower. The first steps seemed easy. My two-year old could climb with minimal assistance. The one-year old needed help on every step. Providential for us all, I always held one hand of each child. We climbed the first three levels with relative ease.

Upon starting the fourth level, I noticed that the children were very tired and having a hard time maintaining their balance. I could not let go of them to wave to my wife, letting her know that everything was hunky dory. In retrospect, I don't think she would have been impressed.

We began to climb the fourth level. Looking up, I could see an open square hole where the stairs ended at the top floor. I am sure that at this point my entire family's guardian angels were flying crazily around the tower. Their arms most likely were wide open waiting to catch whomever they could.

About halfway up the last level, a parent's worst nightmare became reality. My youngest son slipped through the space between two steps. He was dangling in mid-air. Holding my older son with my left hand, I pulled my younger son back up through the hole. As I stood him on the next step, I turned to my oldest son to see if he was out of harm's way. He wasn't. He was slipping off the side of the tower. I held on tight as he fell into open space. My action of turning also pulled my youngest son to the edge where he also slipped off the side of the tower. With both kids dangling off the side and their lives dependent on my actions, I only could hope that my wife was not seeing this. Later, I learned that she had.

Which one do I save first? I decided to rescue my oldest son first since he could understand commands enough to be of some help. The youngest child was light enough that I could hold on to him for some time. I told my two year old to swing to the side where he could catch his foot onto a step. So much for commands; he was petrified.

It was at this point that I completely disagreed with myself—this climb was not a good idea.

I asked God to help me fix this mess. I swung my two year old as best I could toward the steps. His body thumped against the tower as I lifted him up onto the steps. I dared not leave him to sit on the steps as I saved his brother. Then, I felt an inner strength as I scooted my oldest to the side of the tower steps. One dangling child saved.

After that, I was able to pull my youngest straight up and onto the steps. Second dangling child saved.

I thought that it wasn't a bad idea for us to stay there for the rest of our lives.

Then, I tried to gain support for the idea of climbing the few steps that remained to reach our goal. My boys would have nothing to do with it. They wanted down. Bowing to sanity, I gingerly led both boys back down the tower. At the bottom, I let go of them to run to their mother. My arms felt so very long.

My wife did see everything. Feeling helpless with the baby, she prayed. God was with us that day.

Brutal Attack Over TV

Have you ever been hopelessly outnumbered, attacked by persons intent to kill you? I have. This is another story where foolishly I trod.

This happened during a time when I had taken two years off from college to support my wife as she completed her nursing degree. During this period, I became an assistant manager of a loan company. The loan business was pretty straightforward; get people in debt in order to make money.

I would balance any negative ethical considerations by constantly advising our customers to keep their payments up to date and to pay more if they could to pay off a given loan. My responsibilities included the training of new personnel.

It was a hot July afternoon in Indianapolis. That afternoon, I brought a trainee with me to repossess a console television set. The family had an installment loan that was overdue—unpaid for four months. The family lived in a ghetto area just north of the center of the city.

The only parking place I could find was two blocks up the street and one block over. We walked up to the family's house and met the wife, who was a co-signer. We attempted to work out some arrangements where the family could keep the TV. She would not help, deferring any resolution to her husband. We finally agreed that we would remove the TV and keep it in our office until improved financial arrangements could be worked out.

My assistant and I carried the set to the side of the street in front of the family's house. We waited for a van to come and pick it up. As we waited, I thought that everything was going fine until, unexpectedly, the husband came home from work. He was not happy to see us standing in front of his house with his television. I began to explain our position as several of his friends gathered around us. It was at this point that I never saw my assistant again.

As we hashed out the issues, more and more of the man's friends gathered. I thought, "Boy, he sure has a lot of friends." It seemed that there were three or four concentric rings of irate men standing around me. I was doomed.

Someone slashed me with a razor blade attached to a wooden dowel stick. It felt like a prick as it sliced my shirt open. The sight of blood set off frenzy among the spectators. Several others slashed me with razor blades. Someone stabbed me in the upper right chest with a knife. I thought, "Why were they doing this? Am I going to die?"

Having a little wit about me, I bolted and ran. Running was something I could do, bleeding or not. Although some of the crowd ran after me, I easily outran them due to my track experience. Luckily, my car was out of sight and I was so far ahead of my attackers that they did not see me get into my car.

I drove to the office. At the sight of me covered in blood, the staff was petrified. One of my coworkers drove me to the emergency room. They stopped the bleeding from my chest wound and stitched it up. Butterfly bandages were placed over many of the razorblade cuts. After all that, my coworker drove me back to the office. Under advice from my office manager, I left for home to spend three to four days recuperating.

I got into my car and drove myself home. My wife was home to meet me. My torn, blood-soaked shirt and the extent of my wounds stunned her. Being almost finished with her nursing degree, she quickly determined that my wounds were not life threatening.

During my period of recovery, I wrestled with a serious moral dilemma. Did I do what was right? It seemed that "might made right" and I lost by relying on my negotiating skills. Why didn't my logical counseling prevail? I decided that it was best for me to go back to college.

The office manager had the Sheriff reprocess the TV, although it had been broken beyond repair. He wanted me to press charges. Recognizing that the husband knew my name and could find out where I lived, I did not pursue the matter further.

To this day, I still struggle to figure out why I lost the battle over that TV. Why didn't my reasoned approach hold sway? At the time, I remember asking God to help me figure it out. He hasn't answered, at least to my knowledge. Maybe, had that attack not happened, I would not have gone back to college.

Diatoms Under Water

We are so pompous aren't we? We think that we know or can find out all there is to know about anything. We are even so pretentious that we form opinions about the nature of things or events and consider them to be the ultimate truth, even to the point of excluding immeasurable data that substantiate an alternative view. This is even the case in the scientific community.

I have always loved nature, so a natural outcome was preparation for a professional career in natural science. I first became interested in diatoms as an undergraduate in parasitology. During a laboratory session, when we examined fecal material from

Puerto Rico, I noticed numerous tiny transparent objects. The laboratory instructor said that they were diatoms.

Diatoms are common in untreated water. They are a group of microscopic algae that live in cases made of silica. The transparent silica shells pass unharmed through the digestive tract while acids digest the organic parts. They were beautiful in their design, yet diverse in form. I thought at the time that they would be interesting to study with respect to their diversity in various aquatic habitats.

There are many different kinds of diatoms. The diatoms I chose to study live mostly as single organisms attached to surfaces in a stream such as rocks, sunken logs, and the like, as opposed to free floating.

As an extension of this, in graduate school at Indiana University, I decided to major in Limnology, the science of the physical, chemical, and biological aspects of freshwater. In one of the optional laboratory projects, I compared the diatoms found on glass slides submersed in pools with those in riffles where the water is swift.

I realized that there were hundreds of species and many thousands of individual diatoms settling on a small area of a glass slide within a short period of time. Since I also was taking a class in advanced statistics I applied that to the research and realized that when diatom colonies were examined statistically, predictions would be very certain since we had so much sample data.

Soon after, I found myself at the Academy of Natural Sciences in Philadelphia under a fellowship to learn diatom taxonomy from actual specimens used to name various species. This led me to be noticed. Soon, I had a number of fellowships available to me to embark on a Ph.D. curriculum. I applied to a number of schools. Since the University of Delaware accepted me first, I chose that school to major in a new area: that which we now call environmental science. I called it the study of abnormal ecology, because it focused on the altering of natural aquatic systems due to water pollution.

Since I wanted to combine the best courses relevant to my area of study, over a two year period, I worked with or obtained advisors from Yale, Princeton, the University of Pennsylvania, the University of Delaware, and the Academy. I also obtained business guidance from the Harvard School of Business.

My Ph.D. advisory committee was comprised of world renowned professors representing the areas of Ecological Statistics, Diatom Taxonomy, Limnology, Stream Ecology, and Biochemistry. The committee was the crème de la crème of the scientific world. With my fellowship funds, I had almost unlimited resources to pursue my coursework and research. I decided to collect my research data during my first year and analyze it during my second year while I completed my courses and comprehensive exams.

My research centered on verification of widely accepted ideas of how organisms lay claim to new areas. These ideas were universal in that they were true for newly emerging landmasses as well as for barren areas destroyed by fire or volcanic action as well as small cleared areas of jungle. I would show that notions about the roles of initial colonizing species, opportunistic species, competition among species, and the establishment of stable communities were indeed true, as demonstrated through real-time observation.

I would be the first person ever to look under water using a microscope to view first hand what happens when living organisms inhabit new areas. I would document what happened in the first few seconds, minutes, hours, days, weeks, and all seasons over a 12-month period. I would stand alongside the best scientific minds in history: Leewenhook, Darwin, Hutchinson (father of Limnology), and other notables. My star was at its zenith.

My first experiments took place within a 24-hour period alongside a small, undisturbed stream in central Pennsylvania. The location was inside the newly established Stroud Water Research Center administered by the Academy of Natural Sciences of Philadelphia. The location was remote and void of any amenities. My mobile encampment (tent, lights, water laboratory) and microscope were powered by batteries.

It was just nature and me. I felt like Thoreau at Walden Pond. White-tailed deer watched as I went about my silent business. Darkness settled in as I began to observe my sterile glass slides submerged in the stream. Banks of small mechanical counters lining the edge of a wooden board stood at the ready. Each counter would be used to tally a specific diatom known to be common at this site. Others would be tallied by marks on a waterproofed sheet of paper.

I began my first observation. Hand on the board of counters, I placed my first sterilized glass slide under my water emersion lens. Nothing happened. The first couple of seconds seemed like an eternity as I waited for the first expected diatom to appear. I could not wait to get back to my renowned advisory committee to show them my results.

Third second, fourth second—still nothing. Then something happened that I will never forget. My microscope went dark. I checked the power and all was fine. I glanced at the end of the microscope lens. Everything seemed normal. I switched to a lens with a lower magnification. I could not believe my eyes. A big stick seemed to be stuck on my slide!

Since I knew "all there is to know about water," I knew immediately that it was a hyphal strand of a little studied form of fungi, known as "Imperfect Fungi." Where were my diatoms?

I decided to keep observing. Suddenly, a diatom appeared in sight. It became lodged against the stick. Then another stuck against the strand. The strand itself extended and branched. In the process, it caught other diatoms. What was happening? The diatoms were supposed to be deliberately settling on the glass slide, interacting and forming colonies. What was expected to happen wasn't happening at all.

I felt helpless as more and more diatoms became trapped in the growing fungal network. This wasn't dynamics of interactive colonizers. It amounted only to the process of powerless particles being trapped within an ever-expanding web.

I felt destroyed. Everything I had learned from scientific publications or had been taught was wide of the mark. How was I going to explain this? Was my life over as a budding, scientific luminary?

Then the "ah-ha" moment struck. This was the way it was, and it was quite ingenious. If one wanted to collect small things in an efficient manner, a web like the fungal network would be the way to go. I distinctly remember saying, "So, this is the way You do it! It is quite elegant." As the diatoms accumulated on the slide, I was viewing God's creation first hand as it unfolded in real time. Truly, I was in awe of God's handiwork.

It is said to be poor form for a scientist to mix his religious conviction with his work. During my career, I have talked with a number of Nobel laureates and renowned experimental scientists who see God in their work. At the cutting edge of research, scientists see the wonder of how God is at work in the universe. It is the hand of God that is at the foundation of physics, astronomy, biology, and so on. They also are in wonderment of the natural processes that they study.

For me, it was a special night next to that small stream. God and I shared a special look at the natural world. I explained my research findings for what they were, no more and no less. It was new information for those future scientists that followed. My research was acclaimed. The facts were provided by God.

Students on Earth Day

In the spring of 1970, I was in the middle of my first year as an assistant professor and burdened with the preparation and delivery of several new courses. I was not into the vim and vigor of the new environmental movement even when I was looked upon as being an expert in the field.

The first "Earth Day" was planned with a lot of energy and spirit on campuses throughout the country. I was asked to speak at Indiana State University where I was teaching. My assignment was to give a "motivational environmental speech." It was to be given before an assembly of students in the university's new football stadium. What I wanted to do was to show them, by way of projection slides, what the environment was all about and its wonders from the smallest bacteria and algae to the largest ecosystems, hopefully inspiring many to follow in my footsteps.

My plan was to use some 8 x 10 inch photographs of imperfect fungi on glass slides, which had been submerged in a local stream. I gave them to our newly created audiovisual department and simply asked that they be made into projection slides. They took such a considerable amount of time completing the task that I received them just before my presentation. When I looked at them on a projector screen, I was aghast to see nicely made pictures of pieces of paper with photographs on them. I used them anyway.

When I got to the stadium, I saw huge screens where the pictures would be displayed. The stadium was filled with thousands of students. Many were seated, but many were also milling around in a boisterous party spirit. I guess they were ready for football.

I asked God, "Please help me to get through this and in the process show some students a path to make a positive difference in this world." I think my plea was beginning to be answered immediately when I dropped a carousal of slides, spilling them in onto the ground. Loading them into the carousal in the correct order, facing right side front and top side up, took a long time under optimal conditions. Now, I had only a few minutes to put them back into the carousel from a scattered pile on my lap—while sitting in a seat in the bleachers.

While waiting to give my talk, I noted students were celebrating a field day, perhaps an early May Day. They were very loud, unruly, and drowning out the current speaker. I was faced with the seemingly impossible task of giving a serious talk to a crowd of seven thousand people who would rather have a rock concert break out, or a football game. This was not a "speech" crowd. No way would I get and hold their attention. Even those who wanted to listen would not be able to hear me.

All too soon, I was introduced briefly by someone who quickly fled the high platform I stood on. I stood on that platform, overlooking the crowd, I imagined how a Roman emperor might have felt, surveying the multitude—before the lions were let loose.

What followed was what I still feel to this day was a miracle. Suddenly, all of the noise, rowdiness, and milling just about stopped. There was complete silence as thousands of students waited for me to say something. I was spellbound by the stillness, but I knew that God had given me a moment to seize.

I don't remember what I said. I know that I showed a lot of pretty pictures of microscopic life, diverse communities of organisms, and towering vistas. Included were those pictures of pieces of paper and statistical graphs. All were in order. I spoke for almost an hour.

My echo could be heard throughout the stadium. There were no competing sounds. At the end of my talk, there was a standing ovation. I did my job, with the help of God.

Student Crossing the Room

This is about one of the most frightening moments of my life. I almost killed an innocent human being. It happened at a university student and teacher mixer where I taught.

Many students and teachers were in the large meeting room, cleared of chairs. I was alone in a corner, standing with a glass of soda in my hand. In the far corner of the room, I noticed a student who had dropped out of one of my classes. He was about my height, unshaven, and his long hair was disheveled and unkempt. His whole demeanor was creepy. Worse, I had heard that he was "mentally imbalanced" and had provoked many fights.

He started walking toward me with his eyes transfixed, locked on my position in the room. He weaved his way through the crowd, always staring at me. Closer and closer he came. Danger signals were going off in my head. This guy was planning to harm me in some way.

Why was he doing this? Did he drop my class because I was too harsh on him? Was he unable to graduate after dropping my course? A thousand reasons for his behavior rushed through my head.

I took my Marine Corps instruction to heart. If threatened, I was trained to kill, not only with firearms, but also with my hands. I knew that if he came within three feet of me, I would be ready to do whatever was necessary. I would not be able to stop myself. I asked God to protect him from me. I also asked God to protect me. He kept coming, ten feet, five feet, and then four feet.

Just at the very last moment, when he was a mere three feet from me, he veered off and exited the room. I was left trembling and my knees felt weak.

My Marine Corps instincts had nearly kicked in. I could have hurt him badly, possible killed him.

There have been other times when students, pals fooling around, and strangers have neared my personal space. I was able to control myself, save for being somewhat unsettled. Once, during a family walk in the forest, one of my stepdaughters suddenly jumped on my back. My instincts kicked in and I flipped her over my shoulder—toward a steep ravine. I quickly realized who I had and was able to hold onto her. But by doing so, I caused her slight injury.

It has been over fifty years since I left active duty, but still click into "combat mode" at the sound of a popped balloon. Feeling the concussive pressure before hearing the sound, it feels as if I triggered an explosive device. I still "gird up" myself whenever I give my grandchildren balloons. As soon as the balloons begin to loose their buoyancy and sink toward the floor, I take them to a wastebasket and break them.

Though I was never in mortal combat, military training can stick for a lifetime. Sometimes, I feel extremely fortunate not to have seriously injured anyone. I ask God over and over to help me control these deeply ingrained urges gained from my Corps training.

Angel in the Woods

This story could also be titled, "You Are Not Alone." At one point in my career, I led an interagency committee on energy and the environment and the Congressional Research Service labeled me as a "leading environmental scientist."

I was invited by the State of Kentucky to participate in a public forum to provide information on the health and environmental aspects of a proposed coal gasification plant beside the Ohio River. It would be a large, sprawling complex in the flood plain where coal is near the surface.

The planned facility was controversial. The technology was new, considered potentially hazardous, and relatively unproven under commercial conditions. Construction would displace many historic, family-owned farms—land on which these families had lived for several generations

The meeting was held in a room with room enough for about two hundred people, with closed circuit TV feeding two adjacent rooms. The forum also was aired by means of cable to nearby communities.

Ahead of me on the agenda was a representative of the Department of Energy, who spoke on the issue of economics. As he ended his discussion on the topic of improving the local economy, he gave a long list of acronyms and alphanumerical address information.

The crowd became agitated. The farmers in the room were fed up with perceived gibberish and double-talk. Many shouted and a few stood and advanced toward the podium. Guards moved forward to position themselves between the crowd and the speaker. Several guards escorted the Department of Energy speaker out of the room. I was next up to speak.

To say the room was tense is an understatement. I felt as if I was facing a mob armed with torches and pitchforks. My topic was not one conducive to calming their fears. They were clearly expecting to hear hogwash and poised to pounce.

I started out by saying, "You better listen to this. This is important to you. Are you ready? This is the only time I will say this." I then proceeded to tell them a telephone number. I had their attention.

"This is my personal telephone number. It is not that of my secretary or of any central operator. If you call this number, you will get me, no one else, and I will help you personally."

This information and the personal nature in which it was shared appeared to disarm the mob, at least for the time being.

I made a daring move. I said, "I'm going to tell you about all of the health and environmental concerns of this proposed facility. I'll tell you about pollutants that could cause birth defects, cancer, and neurological problems. I'll tell you about controlled and uncontrolled emissions, including what we know and don't know."

I thought that these statements would quell any unrest and have them on the edge of their seats, ready to listen to what I had to say. It did the trick.

I went on to tell them the entire account of how pollutants were created and how they were to be controlled and thoroughly monitored. I was truthful, instilling a sense of trust that the very best science was being brought to bear and that there was no intention to place anyone at risk. The plant would be shut down if there was any indication of a problem. Representatives of the community would be on an oversight board.

After the hour-long presentation, there was no hostility. Apparently, I had worn them out with information they thought they wanted. In the end, they just wanted to feel that it would be safe. Finally, they seemed to trust me to the point that if I thought it would be okay, it was all right with them.

My talk ended the meeting. I packed my briefcase and stood at the rear of the stage while reporters interviewed state officials and politicians as the crowd dispersed. Then, I left by a side door, got in my rental car, and drove back to my motel room across the Ohio River in Indiana.

So, where was God in all of this? Well, in retrospect, He is everywhere and certainly was watching over everything. This reality was not apparent to me until the next day.

In the morning, I had several hours of downtime before I had to be at the airport. I decided to explore a large forest preserve located along the river, in Indiana. Being an ecologist, this was a real indulgence.

I walked into the wilderness for about two miles along a deer trail. Seeing no one, it was great to commune with nature, observing all of the birds and trees I consider friends.

I saw ahead of me what appeared to be an old woman, sitting on a log. As I drew closer, I could see she had her back to me. She was bent over, wearing a shawl over her head, and a long ragged coat.

I thought that it was strange to see her there. There were no houses nearby. To get there, she also had to walk for miles.

As I passed her on the path, she turned her head toward me. Her face was wrinkled and drawn. I did not recognize her. In a soft voice, she said, "You did good last night." Wow! This was a shocker. What was I to say?

Many things went through my mind. Where did she come from? What was she doing there? In this moment in time and place, is this real? Did she see me on television? How could she recognize me so fast? Was she waiting for me?

I simply said, "Thank you," and continued to walk down the path.

About thirty-five feet from the log, I turned around to see what she was doing. She was not there. She had seemingly disappeared into thin air. There was nowhere for her to go.

As a scientist, I have no earthly explanation of what happened. This is a case where something tangible went "poof" and was gone.

Was she an angel? Was she a messenger from God? Was she God? Was there more to her message than "you did good," perhaps a deeper meaning? Did I need to hear the message? Was it to inspire me to do more? Was it merely a "Thank you?" Why an old woman?

For many years, I have thought of what happened. In truth, I don't have an answer. The old woman did not look like anyone I knew or have come to know since that day. My closest explanation is that she represented the downtrodden. She symbolized those that have been disenfranchised and bullied by government and society. That is, she was a collective image of those ancestral farmers of the Ohio floodplain. In essence the message was, "Finally someone has listened to us."

I don't think that the message and its uncanny presentation changed my life. Maybe it was not intended to do so. I have accepted it as it was. My only regret is that I did not add, "I'm glad I could help".

What did I do immediately after she disappeared? I continued down the path, making a large loop back to my car. Yes, I continued to look back. Each time, ever more distant, I only saw the log.

What happened to the coal gasification plant? A change in economic conditions led to project cancellation.

Mayor in Malaysia

In 1978, I was asked to help plan Malaysia's environmental program and incorporate it into the country's five-year economic plan. About a month before I left, I visited an arts and crafts fair sponsored by the City of Fairfax, Virginia. I wonder, even over 30 years later, why I went.

The annual fair is out of the way from my normal travels. For me, such fairs are hard on my feet and rather mind numbing due to the huge number of monotonous exhibits. My wife and children were with me, although it wasn't an event conducive for sustaining the attention of kids. Usually such trips are taken on my initiative. There always were closer arts and crafts fairs. Anyway, its still a puzzler why we went to this Fairfax fair.

We were browsing through various tents when I stopped in one displaying handmade jewelry and clothes. The early middle-aged woman who operated the booth had two small children in tow. My interest focused on her beautiful necklace. It was long, with a number of large and small colored beads. It held a delicate floral pendant. I asked her where the inspiration for her work came from. She said, "Malaysia."

I said that I would be leaving for Malaysia in a few weeks. She unexpectedly said, "Tell my father that I am fine." Then she told me his name which I could not understand and which I quickly forgot. I said, "Sure." She smiled and I left. I could have said under my breath, "Fat chance." But just the opposite, I felt caught up in a feeling of an inescapable journey and purpose.

Time passed and I eventually found myself in Malaysia, engrossed in the exotic and complex affairs of the Malaysian way of life. First, we addressed all of the country's Sultans or their representatives in a large meeting hall. They were required to assist us in our endeavor. I presented a three-hour talk on how the United States developed its environmental laws and regulations. They were engrossed in my presentation, which usually would be quite boring. I livened it up with a lot of pictures and colored charts.

About halfway through the talk, the Malaysian facilitator came to the microphone, broke into my presentation, and said some words in Malaysian. At that point, the entire audience left the conference room. It was very disconcerting and I remember saying to myself, "Was it something I said?" I decided to follow the crowd out of the room. I found all of the attendees facing tables lining a long hallway. They were gesturing, making loud noises, and holding ceramic cups in their hands. It was teatime. The tea had to be consumed before it cooled.

About a week later, after having developed a draft environmental program and its justification within an economic context, I found myself on the road within the country. As a guest, I could go wherever I liked. I wanted to get out into the interior jungles to see everyday jungle life.

One of the country's mottos was, "Behind every rubber tree is a man and behind him is his family and behind his family is his country." It was an inspirational slogan to depict how important the rubber industry was to the economic prosperity of the country. The country also was diversifying into palm oil and local village-based batik production. I wanted to get out into the boondocks to see this for myself.

My guide, from the Ministry of Forestry, took me deep into the Malay Peninsula. Hidden within the jungle were tiny hamlets, each inhabited by a mayor and a number of families. Each village focused on raw rubber production. Also, each had several large vats used to dye white cloth into exquisite Malaysian cloths having intricate multi-colored designs.

We came into one such jungle hamlet. Waiting for me in the center of the village was the mayor. He stood before a large, rectangular building on high stilts. This was his simple home. He welcomed me in. We climbed steep steps, took off our shoes, and entered the single large room. He gestured for me to sit down on a chair on one side of the room. My guide sat several feet to my right. The mayor sat to my left on another side of the room.

We sat in silence. I realized that it was an honor for him to be visited by an "important" person from such an "important" country. We shared our companionship without saying a word.

Being rambunctious, I am not one for accepting the status quo. I noticed a number of pictures above where the mayor sat and stood up to go look at them. I must have broken some sort of protocol rule because my guide stood up and tried to stop me. The mayor motioned for him to sit down.

I began to look at the pictures as the mayor moved beside me. My eyes focused on one particular picture of an attractive, familiar-looking young woman wearing a long, beaded necklace supporting a delicate floral pendant. In broken English, the mayor said that she was his daughter and that, "She left many years ago and now lives in the United States. Is she alright?" I told him, "Yes, I saw her a few weeks ago. She is fine." He nodded his head and with sincere contentment said, "Thank You."

Yes, God works in mysterious ways. Sometimes we are instruments in His plans without even knowing it. Lucky are we who are able to see His works.

Aborigine

While traveling deep within the Malayan jungles, my guide wanted me to see a government project involving jungle clearing and native relocation and training. We came upon one such development that was very striking. It was void of vegetation for miles where the mountainous native jungle was clear-cut.

The local aboriginal population had been moved to the fringes of the cleared area. The bare land was being prepared for the growing of oil palms, creating a new and stable source of income for the native inhabitants.

We visited one aborigine at the edge of the jungle. He and his wife and children lived in a modest bamboo hut. Although under pressure by the government to "modernize," he stubbornly clung to traditional housing. He built a system of bamboo pipes to carry water from a mountain spring directly into his home. He had a continuous source of cool running water.

The aborigine wanted to show me the source of his water supply. My guide did not want to climb the mountain, so off we went on our adventure. With blowgun in hand, he led me upward along a narrow path bordering his bamboo conduit. I heard a cacophony of familiar sounds. I realized it was what I had heard in old Tarzan films!

When we reached the top of the trail, I could see a clear bubbling spring supplying his personal "aqueduct". Above in the trees, he spied a small monkey, which he speedily stunned with a dart from his blowgun. He placed it in his knapsack to take home for his wife to suckle until it was old enough to be eaten.

In the soft soil near the spring, I saw fresh footprints of a small tiger. Even though educated in the "modern world," I knew that wherever there is a baby tiger, the mother would not be far away. This fact was verified when I showed my new aborigine friend the footprints. His consternation was apparent, even without a translator. He swiftly led me down the path.

Back at his hut, his family gathered around their hunter-gatherer hero. I wondered who had it the better— us in our amenity-laden world, or my new friend in his "primitive" environment. I know we long for the loving support of such a "nuclear" family.

There in the jungle, it seemed God had transcended the barrier between the so-called terms of modern/primitive, foreigner, gentile, sinner, infidel, outsider, non-believer, and the like.

My new aborigine friend represented the "nobility of man." I understood that God is more universal than our understanding that He is only for the "righteous." Later, back at my home, I felt compelled and inspired to write the following prose.

On a visit to an aborigine home

I did not plan to meet you,
    so you came into my life by surprise.
I was not prepared for your world.

You were given a new house and land close to your native home
    and you do not seem to mind.

All this is superficial,
    as I see through your faceless expressions.

I understand your pride in hunting with blowgun and spear,
    building with bamboo and palm,
    and planting rice to justify your keep.

I see your wit and quick mind,
>   determined to be unsurpassed.

I see in you what most of mankind has lost,
>   the nobility of man.

I wish you well.

(Upon a visit to the home of a relocated Malaysian aborigine, 1978)

Deadly Oil Palms

Sometimes, I think that my rash actions will get me killed. With the help of a guardian angel, maybe many guardian angels, I can't count how many times I had been saved by the grace of God. This is an example.

One of the many places I visited in Malaysia was an oil palm plantation. At these plantations, oil is extracted from the nuts of oil palms and used for many purposes. (Remember Palmolive oil?) The nuts are collected from groves of palms and transported to an onsite processing plant where they are de-husked and pressed, thereby releasing the oil.

I decided I wanted to get a close look at the palm trees. I climbed down an embankment surrounding a five-acre grove and began to take pictures of clusters of nuts on the trees. Standing on the bank were many plantation workers and representatives of the government who regulated the industry. They were all waving at me. I thought that it was a courteous gesture, so I waved back. I thought, "These really are friendly folks." I kept taking pictures.

When I climbed back out of the embankment, I was eagerly greeted with hugs and pats on the back by the workers and officials. This seemed like an unusually friendly behavior for Malaysians. That is when they let me know of the dangerous predicament I had unwittingly put myself into.

It turns out the plantation workers release cobras into the groves to control rodents. Yes, cobras.

Before workers enter the groves for harvesting, they flood the groves to kill the cobras. How many cobras were around me? I don't know. I was looking high at clusters of palm nuts. By accounts all around,

I should have been bitten many times. Yes, I guess angels do watch over fools.

Bay of Bengal

There is a saying, "No man is an island." That is, we don't live our lives alone, but within a context that may include family, friends, or others who care for us, or depend on us. With all the hustle and bustle of the modern world, we often search for any modicum of solitude. At other times, we find a little too much solitude. Such was the case with my visit to Sri Lanka.

On my way back from Malaysia, I decided to spend some time in Sri Lanka. I would have no guide and was intent on being a stranger in a strange land. My intent was to continue to Madras, India, but my assigned airplane broke its tail off entering a hangar, resulting in a prolonged stay. Sri Lanka, in the late 1970's was outwardly peaceful, without uninhibited conflict between the Government and the Tamil Rebels.

I visited silver mines in the mountainous interior, the festival city of Kandy, broad wetlands, the ocean, and a resort with a veranda overlooking the focus of the film "Bridge on the River Kwai." English was spoken everywhere, so I didn't feel like a stranger.

It was at the ocean where I felt most alone. I went for a stroll along the surf of the Bay of Bengal near Sri Lanka's capital city of Colombo. Actually, the location is on the Indian Ocean, not on the Bay of Bengal which lies on the east side of Sri Lanka. I use the latter term because it sounds more exotic.

It was after dark and no one else was on the beach. A slight breeze blew onshore. I began to wonder why I was there so very far from home and why I was beginning to feel isolated. It was just the sea, the beach, and me, reflecting on the meaning of life.

Offshore, I could see tiny flickers of light. Sometimes I could see a light, sometimes not. I became aware that the lights were small lanterns carried by fishermen in little one-man boats. As the fishermen rowed, they would dip within an ocean swell, becoming unseen from land.

I began to feel a kinship with my unknown friends. I began to wonder who was more alone, me standing alone on the shore or them alone in their small boats. To some extent, we all are alone in this world as we move through our life on earth. God is watching and we can talk to Him anytime we want. We are not in heaven, but at times like that, on that beach, we can really feel the presence of God.

I said farewell to my brothers at sea and walked back to my hotel. I sat down and wrote the following.

Watching the lights of fishermen in the
Bay of Bengal

My friends, you fishermen,
    I have been watching you for some time,
    you in your small boats on such a dark night.

One, Two, Three ... Ten,
    I barely see your flickering lights as you dip
    among the swells.

The wind is strong and I worry for your safety,
    you seem so far away.

I, alone, also feel the breeze, strong as it is.
You with the sea and I here on land,
    I wonder who is safer.

You, too, are alone,
    but safe from the trials and maelstrom of the land,
    just you, the fish, and the sea.

Me with a myriad of temptations and fears,
    on the contrary for you, life is simple,
    one, but important threat … the sea.
For me life is not simple and I wish it were.

I am sure you love the sea, my friends,
    and would not change places,
    nor would I.

I shall miss you.

(Standing at night on a beach near Colombo,
Sri Lanka, 1978)

Elephants in Sri Lanka

In 1949, during my fifth year of elementary school, my family moved from Chicago to rural Indiana. The difficulty was not so much fitting into a new environment as it was enduring the shenanigans perpetrated on me by girls in my class. Their love for hiding my books, throwing my papers on the floor, or teasing me, was only surpassed by their superiority antics inflicted during sixth and seventh grades. Thank goodness, decency prevailed throughout high school.

For an eleven year old, dreams of faraway places were an excellent means of escapism. I became isolated as much as possible. I read books, did homework at school, and immersed myself in schoolwork.

One of my favorite courses of study was geography. It brimmed with exciting adventure and exotic, far-away locales.

One day, our geography teacher told us to turn to the section of our textbook on Southeast Asia. I recall a black and white picture of local people washing elephants in a stream in Ceylon (now called Sri Lanka). The picture depicted an exotic land—another world. The people appeared to be friendly, happy, and at one with their environment. It was far out. I visualized being in that distant and strange land. At home, I often would open the book and stare at the picture, wishing to travel there some day.

Fast forwarding three decades, I was able to travel to Malaysia to help establish an environmental protection program for the country. While looking at a world map, I saw that I could continue from Malaysia around the world. On the way home, I could stop in Sri Lanka. My childhood dream could come true.

In August, 1978, I left Malaysia and headed home. My itinerary included a layover in Sri Lanka.

Serendipitously, the airplane that was to be my means of continuing to Damascus and London broke its tail off while being towed into a hangar. I would be "stuck" in Sri Lanka for several days.

I carried a copy of the picture from my old textbook, together with a notation citing where the photograph was taken. The site was located about halfway in my travel from the capital city of Colombo on the Indian Ocean to the centrally located historic city of Kandy. The location was easy to find. Upon approaching the river, I could see people washing elephants just as in my picture. I took my own pictures and shared my story with everyone present.

Since that time, I have given motivational talks at elementary schools and high schools. I would challenge students to follow their dreams, just as I did. I would tell my story, showing my old textbook and my pictures. It would be very moving most of the time.

Once during a presentation at a northern Virginia school, I said, "Maybe some day you can travel to a foreign land." Half of the class raised their hands and told of places they had been: Malaysia, Samoa, India, New Zealand, and many other countries were mentioned. After my talk, I learned that many of the parents of the students worked for the U.S. State Department. Nevertheless, I thought it was motivational.

Why do I include this story in this book? I think that my dream fulfillment wasn't just a combination of circumstances or just a happenstance. I think that Divine action was at hand. It was kind of like a "thank you" for hanging in there on that dream for so many years. It was fascinating that the dream of a twelve year old boy could not only stay alive, but grow through the years. Now, over sixty years from its use, I still have that old textbook somewhere.

Gas Transportation Plan

Professionally, I have accomplished many things, but this project was one of those that left me most fulfilled. It involved adventure, politics, ingenuity, and humility in subservience to God.

In 1979, as part of my independent support to the U.S. Environmental Protection Agency, I was asked to provide environmental assistance to the White House in the formulation of the President's decision on the Alaskan Gas Transportation Plan. By statute, the President was required to report to Congress on his approval or non-approval of a strategy to develop and transport natural gas from Alaska, similar to the development and transport of Alaskan oil.

It was a multi-billion dollar venture with many transport options, including air, water, land, and combinations of route scenarios. As a result, the project posed many threats to unique animal and plant communities. With multiple levels of governmental and international jurisdictions involved, a consensus was problematic. My task was to provide advice on the pros and cons of a positive decision based on an environmental point of view.

I needed to understand the aspects of the undertaking. I traveled extensively throughout Alaska, talking to local and state officials, scientists, corporate officials, technicians, local inhabitants, and oil pipeline engineers. I even stood on the deck of the Exxon Valdez where I was made aware of the many safeguards in place to prevent a widespread and devastating oil spill (of course we all know the end of that story—one of the biggest oil spills in history).

I stood on the shore of Prince William Sound at a location untouched by human activities. I examined the Alaskan Oil pipeline and development operations at Prudhoe Bay. I studied the frail wetland drainage patterns of the Alaskan National Wildlife Refuge (ANWR).

Although intentionally trained in ecological sciences, I have never claimed to be an "environmentalist" or "eco-freak." I believe in "environmental compatibility", that economic development can occur without significantly degrading natural systems. In fact, development can take place in a way that enhances the stability and diversity of natural systems.

The planning for such a course of development takes a lot of innovative thinking and negotiation to achieve a win-win for both sides, but it can happen. One of the downsides of being the man–in-the-middle in such situations is that no one likes you and the position of all involved is to thwart your efforts. It takes a tough skin to stay the course, but the reward of a successful outcome is worth the aggravation.

After the data-gathering stage, it was time to start talking. I remember arriving back in Northern

Virginia from Alaska vividly. It was a Saturday evening and I was taking scores of rolls of 35-mm film to a film laboratory in Maryland to be developed and prepared as projection slides. I picked them up on Sunday afternoon and arranged them for a Council on Environmental Quality (CEQ) presentation early Monday morning. The CEQ is the "right arm" for the White House in terms of environmental policy.

It was easy to say that the Alaskan animals and plants were too fragile to allow for encroachment. Wild musk ox, migratory reindeer, polar bear, seal, whale, and waterfowl populations seemed to cry out for protection. How could we allow such a "heavy" implementation of man-induced infringement?

Subsequent to review by the CEQ, I attended a meeting at the old Executive Office Building next to the White House. Members of the cabinet and various White House advisors were present. I presented my findings with regard to the most environmentally acceptable transportation alternative, various environmental concerns, and opportunities for mitigating negative impacts. Discussion quickly reached a consensus on the most appropriate transportation route based on economic and environmental factors.

The core issue needing resolution was how oversight was to be managed amongst competing local and governmental environmental authorities. How would permit applications be reviewed among the various agencies? Which agency would have primary jurisdiction? Within the executive branch itself, would the Department of Transportation, Labor, Interior, Energy, Commerce, or the Environmental Protection Agency have the most influence over permitting priorities? Without consensus, this single issue created a roadblock to reaching a White House decision. By law, the President was to report his decision to Congress within two days. The meeting was to reconvene the next day.

I felt downcast, disappointed because I was unable to provide a reasoned resolution to the impasse. As one who had been in the trenches over the decision, I felt that I should be able to provide an insightful way out of the deadlock. I went home that day racking my brain. Even though no one else could offer a logical proposal, why couldn't I? I was supposed to be the intellectual, the environmental professional, the know-it-all. I felt that I had let the President and Congress down.

I had a fitful night, tossing and turning. I lay in bed, trying to find an answer, yet I knew I needed sleep to be sharp and alert for the next day's meeting. I was mad at myself. I questioned if I should be involved in the decision-making process. I felt I was in way over my head. Finally, I said, "Dear God, I've done all I can. I can do no more. It is in your hands. Please help us find an answer." Then, I fell asleep.

I don't dream. In any case, I don't dream in specifics. I dream in colors, images, and the like. I hardly ever remember anything from my slumber. This night was different.

At some point in the dark night, a bright, clear, and detailed illustration came into view. It was a diagram of the relationship of all of the competing agencies and organizational entities and how they could interact through the single office of "Federal Inspector." This independent office would coordinate permit reviews, thereby assigning priorities and expediting the permitting process. The office would keep everyone in the information loop. The image was so obvious, yet specific enough to be implemental.

I forced myself to wake up. I had to write this down. I knew that I would not be able to remember it in the morning. On an end table beside my bed, I took a sheet of typing paper and drew the diagram exactly as it was in my dream. Then, I quickly fell asleep, though I could hardly wait to wake up.

I awoke early, feeling well rested. I glanced to the table and saw my well-designed drawing of a simple bureaucracy—a solution to the President's problem. I immediately took the sketch to my home computer where I reproduced it using a simple graphics program. I printed it. With my copy in hand, I rushed out the door for the White House. On my way, I thanked God for His gift.

At the White House meeting, everyone quickly reached agreement that this solution was the best idea since buttered toast. Each Cabinet member wanted to claim it as his own idea. Having been given the primary leadership role under the governing statute, the Secretary of Transportation took the recommendation to the President for his signature and transmittal to Congress. That recommendation, including my God-inspired diagram, remains in the Congressional archives.

As a postscript, the Alaskan Gas Transportation System was never implemented due to economic reasons. However, the office of the Federal Inspector has since been realized and played a crucial role in protecting Alaska's natural resources.

Near Death Experience

Many claim to have had near death experiences. Now, I am one. I've always believed those who had such experiences actually believed they were true. I accepted it as fact that they actually had near death experiences. I learned two things from mine. It happens when you are not expecting it and it affects those around you as much, if not more, than yourself.

My experience occurred in 2002 when I was sixty-four years old. I had a severe bronchial infection and was on antibiotics.

My paternal family health history shows a pattern of recurring respiratory infections. My brother died from complications of such an infection. My father was pronounced dead from the Asiatic flu in World War I and placed in a morgue. When an attendant began to inject embalming fluid into him, my father suddenly took a deep breath, very much alive. The attendant wasn't seen again.

For me, I was actually feeling quite good. I was miserable with the infection, but was able to walk around the house, performing a few minor chores while my wife was working nearby as a church secretary. Since it would be about three hours before she returned home, I decided to lie down on our bed.

My plan was to lie very still. Although I wasn't sleepy, if I would just barely breathe, I thought that I would feel better and time would easily pass. It seemed like a good plan.

Almost immediately after I laid down, I suddenly felt myself rising into some sort of empty space. I definitely felt myself rising. I was shocked to find myself in such a situation. I definitely felt that I was not in my earthly body. I could see myself appearing as a complete spirit appearing as my body, but without substance.

Within a second, I could see my objective. I was rising in the void toward a room protruding from a high place on a non-descript building. The room was located on a corner of the building and it had no outside walls. As I drew closer, I could discern human figures standing at the outside edge of the floor. A light seemed to illuminate the room from a rear corner. It seemed that I was being drawn up rapidly to the room.

I soon realized the figures in the room were relatives, friends, professors, and teachers I knew from my past. In the front row were my brother, an uncle and his wife, my father and mother, a professor, and another uncle. I sensed I knew every one. They looked like they were when I saw them at their best, not at the time of their death. Their commonality was that all were individuals I loved or respected and all had died. I became conscious that they were a welcoming party.

Another realization was that they all were happy, were friends, and even soul mates. Each and every one was truly joyous and full of love. This was not the case in real life. In life they were simple blokes with faults like all of us. They definitely did not appear to be joyous and full of love on earth. Now they were full of unadulterated joy, welcoming me as one of their own.

As I neared the room, the light at the back of the room became brighter. It was emanating from an open door at the rear corner of the room. The light wasn't really blinding, but it was a pure, almost platinum, white light. By pure, I mean that it seemed complete in its spectrum, welcoming, and filled with love—not characteristics of any light I'd ever seen on earth. I was being drawn past the welcoming party and into the light.

Awareness is a strange thing. Like some people who see their entire life before them as they are about to die, awareness comes in an instant. My awareness was that there was no time in the room or behind the open door. I could have been where I was ten thousand earth years ago or a hundred years in the future. Existence in the room and beyond was forever and time did not exist.

Simultaneously, I realized that I did not have to involuntarily enter the room that instant, that day, or any day. I could stay on earth and remain a mainstay to my wife and family. I could choose to continue to help others in my volunteer charity efforts. Abruptly, I found myself back in bed and quite awake.

What does one do after such an experience? I chose to lie still, although bright-eyed, and take stock of my state of affairs. First, I was alive. I definitely was inside my body, which seemed to be shaking, slightly yet rapidly. I had been gone from this earth by clock time for no more than a minute. I was alone. Should I call my wife and tell her what happened? No, I would not need to shock her since I was alive and seemingly without lingering effects — or so I thought.

I decided to get up and walk around. My first sensation was that I was heavy, being drawn to the floor by some strong, unpleasant force called gravity. As I stood up, I saw the corners of the room, the walls, and the bedroom door. Why were they there?

The door was closed. I tried to walk through it—with an awakening jolt. I could not understand why it was there or why any of the confinement of the house was necessary. Now, I surely wasn't going to call my wife immediately. I continued moving though the house and it now seemed so foreign to me and pointless, somehow.

Finally, toward the end of her workday, I called my wife to let her know that I was okay, but needed to talk to her about something bizarre that had happened.

When she arrived home, she was concerned. I was unquestionably "out of it." I recounted my near death, "out of the body" experience. It could seem to her to be just a dream, if it were not for my newfound peculiarities. I would continue to feel the walls of the house, asking her, "Why are they here?" "Why are they solid?" and "Why do we have doors?" It became quite unnerving for her. I assured her that

I could not help to have these feelings and that I really was all right. Based on her apparent fright and minor shaking, I don't think my assurance was all that comforting.

My peculiarities lasted several days and then gradually diminished. My wife admonished me not to tell anyone outright, at least not right away until I "settled down." I was to be careful about questioning the reasons for earthly structures and necessities.

I feel better now. I am earthbound and have grown accustomed to it again. I try not to dwell on life outside my body, lest I relapse. Of course, I feel okay with dying. I know that I will die at some point. I don't know if it will be today, next week, or thirty years from now. I also know that in heaven, it doesn't make any difference. And, I know I am welcome anytime. Today, I am left with an admonishment from my wife, "Stay away from the light."

My Will

Have you ever talked to God? I mean really? That is when He talked back? I have. It's moving, but not all that uplifting in the moment, if one is quaking in his boots as I was.

It was a slow, typical morning. Having gotten up, read the newspaper, bathed, dressed, grabbed something to eat, and driven to church for the 7:45 a.m. service, I was still drowsy. When it came time for communion, my wife and I approached the communion area. As was our custom, she stood and I knelt as we waited for our priests to bring us the consecrated bread and wine.

I was still half-asleep as I petitioned God for help in an almost robotic tone. I really meant what I was saying, but it was methodical to the point of having been committed to memory.

As I knelt, I was praying, "please God, let me be good," "help me to be nice to others," and "help me to do what is right." Then out of the blue God said, "My Will!" He was very emphatic. "You scared me—I didn't mean to make you mad," I replied silently.

The voice I'd heard was definitely male, loud, bottomless, unyielding, and full of meaning. The pronouncement was not simply my own conscience—I knew that voice well. This voice was authoritative and not me. Nor was it that soft feeling one senses as a response to a prayer.

I was just about knocked over by the sound of God's voice. It came into my consciousness without warning. It was abrupt and measurable in nanoseconds. There was no explanation, just those two words. I looked around to see if anyone else heard it, but all seemed normal.

My immediate thoughts were that God was not satisfied. It wasn't enough that I was asking help to do all the right things. In fact, I was asking God to do my will—what I wanted. That was the difference. I was not asking God to do His will. No matter how pious, devout, virtuous, dutiful, decent, or proper I thought my requests might have been, I was asking God to do my will, not His. I was putting myself and my desires before those of God, without so much as knowing it. And, God set me straight without any doubt.

I felt like Saul being struck down by the power of God on the road to Damascus, though glad I hadn't fallen down or out of the communion area. Had I been, what explanation other than the truth could I give? Surely, if the truth had become known, attendance at communion would have likely declined to zero, out of fear that God would smite others down.

I was really shaken up by the experience. It has become somewhat disconcerting to know that God can speak to me at any time. I always knew it could happen, but to have it happen so suddenly and without warning was very disarming. It brings about a realization that each of us is totally vulnerable to God's intrusion into our life. Indeed, we are not masters of our own lives. At the present time, I feel that God is even closer at hand — watching and listening. His ease of access has become accepted and even welcome.

Ian's Interactions with the Spiritual World

I babysat my grandson Ian from when he was two until nine years old. He is ten now. During this stretch of time, we have become very close. We have shared many adventures as we helped low-income families and the homeless. He has grown into a well-rounded, happy fellow, with great academic and social skills. He also has ties to his inner self, his soul, that have formed a spiritual bond between us that transcends our earthly world.

1. Singing "I'll Fly Away"

When Ian was less than two years old, he was sitting with me watching an old-fashioned gospel hour. I looked over at Ian and he was singing the song "I'll Fly Away," in time with the group on TV. He was singing the exact words in a very loud, lively and enthusiastic fashion.

I said to Ian, "How do you know those words? You've never heard it. There is no way you can know it."

He looked at me and said, "uh oh." He knew he had been caught. I said, "You knew that song before you were born. You knew it in heaven, didn't you?" Looking rather chagrined, Ian simply said, "Yes." I asked him if he wasn't supposed to talk about such matters. He said, "I'm not supposed to talk about that."

At that moment, it looked as if the door between heaven and earth had been opened. From that instant, our relationship has never been the same.

We did make use of his newfound singing talent. He went with me to next appearance of our church's

Front Porch Singers. He stood on a tall stool as he belted out the words of "I'll Fly Away" for a group of residents at an elderly care center. Those assembled could not believe that he was only two years old. They were even more impressed by the story behind his song.

In spite of his reservations on speaking out about such matters, Ian has let his guard down since that time and has talked somewhat freely about the spiritual world. Now he has forgotten some of our divine sharing, but not all.

2. Seeing me with the roadrunner

Remember Wile E. Coyote and the Roadrunner? In 1982, I was in Austin, Texas, on business. I had a morning break in meetings and decided to run a couple of miles or so near a lake northwest of town. As I was running on a narrow gravel road, a roadrunner came out of the scrub vegetation next to the road and began to run with me. It ran about 500 yards, staying four feet away on my right side. Then, it abruptly exited back into the bushes.

Twenty years later, when Ian was two years old, I began telling him the story of the roadrunner; he stopped me and said, "I know." I said "No, you don't know the story. I never told it to you." "I saw you running with the roadrunner." He told me in detail how the roadrunner came out of the brush, how it looked, and how it ran beside me.

How could Ian have known this? Was he somehow able to view me or gain knowledge of me back then? His mother was only five years old. Where was Ian anyway? Was he in heaven? Was it destiny way back then that I would eventually be divorced and then marry his future grandmother? Was it providence that Ian and I would become so closely bonded and in tune with the spiritual world?

It was truly a scary moment when Ian told me that he had been watching me. How much more had he seen in my life and for how long? Did he know my every thought, dream, and imperfection? Did he and does he know our future?

I try not to ask too many questions about these matters. If I do ask, it is often indirect. I know that he tends to shut down and avoid talking about his existence before he was born. So, I try not to press any spiritual or mystical quandary. Clearly, the "I'll Fly Away" incident opened a heavenly door. Sadly, that door is beginning to close.

3. Falling on broken beer bottles

It was a beautiful afternoon for a three year old and his grandfather. The sun was shining and the autumn temperature of October was just right. Ian and I had the afternoon to ourselves until his mother returned home from work. It was a perfect time to walk over to our local ice cream parlor.

Ian ran ahead across the entrance to the shopping center. I yelled for him to be careful and to wait for me to catch up. It was at that moment that I saw him trip and fall down on one knee near the curb. I was dismayed to find he had fallen into a pile of broken beer bottles, knee first.

I envisioned a massive amount of blood seeping from his knee as he stood up. Ian slowly stood up, above the pile of glass as I rushed to his side. I was ready to see the blood flowing and already prepared to administer first aid or to get him to a hospital, if needed. His knee was unblemished. Before I could do or say anything, Ian said calmly, "Don't worry Papa, my guardian angel caught me."

There was nothing I could say. He seemed quite unmoved by the mishap. There, before me, was a spotless and healthy knee. We continued walking. His knee was none the worse, although I was a bit shaken by the whole experience.

Today, I feel that Ian's explanation was right on the mark. He unmistakably knew his guardian angel was by his side, keeping him from harm.

4. Stations of the Cross at Shrine Mont

Ian was four years old when I took him on his first trip to Shrine Mont, a mountain retreat complex established almost a century ago by our Episcopal diocese. We hiked up 700 feet in elevation to a cross and tower that overlooked a valley in the Appalachian Mountains.

It was quite a climb for one so young, but he did it like an experienced hiker. On the way back down, we passed a series of Stations of the Cross, pictures that depicted the final hours of the life of Christ.

As we passed one of the pictures that illustrated Christ being nailed to a cross, Ian suddenly stopped. He asked, "What does this mean?" I said that it portrayed Jesus being killed.

Ian was transfixed. He stood directly in front of the wooden panel. His lips were moving slightly; otherwise he stood tall and rigid. I did not know what to do. He was only four. Should I shake him? Should I speak loudly to try to wake him up?

I recalled the scenes of Our Lady of Fatima, when Mary, the mother of Christ, appeared before a simple peasant girl. She also appeared to be spellbound and motionless, except for the slight motion of her lips.

I just stood a few yards downhill from Ian, as if urging him onward. He didn't budge. I became somewhat fidgety and uneasy. We shared that experience for what seemed to be about ten minutes.

Finally, he moved back a step or two and looked at me. I said, "What were you doing?" He said, "I was talking to Jesus." I guess four year old children can do that.

Apparently, when Ian was in heaven, before he was born, he wasn't told or didn't need to know about the crucifixion of Jesus. He was unprepared for what he saw.

Ian said that he asked Jesus what it was all about. He was surprised and shocked to see that there was so much about Jesus that he didn't know. How could I be telling him something so astonishing about Jesus, after he had spent time with Jesus? I asked him if he had any questions. He said, "No." Seemingly, Ian was satisfied with what he was told.

We proceeded down the mountain. Although I had so many questions to ask, I didn't want to interfere with his encounter with God. I felt that we were even more bonded together. I had my knowledge of Jesus that was passed down from oral and written records and he had his firsthand. It seemed to all fit together as we emerged from the deep forest: my knowledge of the New Testament, his talking directly with Jesus, the hallowed retreat, and being surrounded by God's creation.

5. Ian's Vision

One day, when Ian was four, we were riding together in my truck on a normal roundabout. Suddenly, Ian became very tense and said, "My Mommy hurt her hand really bad." I said, "Last week, I think she bumped it." He said, "No, — Now!" I said, "Is it broken? Is she okay?" "Yes." I took it at face value and waited to see if anything happened.

About an hour later, his mother called me on my cell phone and said that she had hurt her hand! She was in a parking lot, and had just opened her car door. A sudden gust of wind blew, whipping the door open, and slamming it against another car, trapping her hand between the cars. I said, "I know." She said, "No, I just hurt it about an hour ago." I said, "It is okay. Ian says that your hand will be alright." I then reported on Ian's vision. There wasn't much she could say.

At 21 months of age, Ian's younger brother Austin, showed similar prowess. She was holding him when he said, "What's that noise?" She said, "It's someone hammering outside." He said, "No—telephone!" A moment later, the telephone rang.

6. Ian's Guardian Angel

Ian's guardian angel has blue wings. He has said this since he was able to talk. Over seven years later, he sticks to his story. And yes, his guardian angel is real. He even introduced me to him one day when his angel was with us. It seems that his guardian angel felt reluctant to visit when I was with Ian unless there was a formal introduction. Ian also has introduced his guardian angel to his grandmother.

I have overheard Ian speaking with his guardian angel. His guardian angel has a family and leaves Ian to visit with them. In recent years, Ian's angel has still dropped in on an occasional basis.

When Ian was three years old, I remember him being downcast for several days because his guardian angel said he would not see him for a long time. Two years later, I asked Ian if he was still sad that he was unable to talk to his guardian angel as often as he would like. He said, "No, I can always talk to Austin's guardian angel."

One day while Austin, Ian, and I were riding in my pickup truck, Ian said, "He's here." I said, "Who?" He said, "Austin's guardian angel is right beside us." Now, I have been formally introduced to Austin's angel.

Once I showed Ian a picture of a blue angel in our church library. It was a typical depiction of an adult winged person. I asked, "Is this what your guardian angel looks like?" Ian, looking very disgusted, said simply and emphatically, "No!"

At what point does one determine that a child is talking to an imaginary friend rather than an angel? I think with time childhood thoughts may prevail over reality. I think that Ian's initial revelations about his guardian angel were real. I can not deny that Ian fell onto broken glass without a mark. His immediate remark that his guardian angel saved him seems to "fit the bill". As Ian grew older, story line blanks seemed to be filled in with creative imagination.

Personally, I believe guardian angels exist. I have not seen Ian's or Austin's, but I have seen one in the woods many years ago. She didn't have wings, but she was real.

Here By the Grace of God

Have you ever thought that you are alive today solely due to the grace of God? Perhaps you have steered clear of a possible car accident or sidestepped a crumbling cliff at the last second. Well, I have no small number of what some people call "strokes of luck." These are a few of my travel stories that, due to my own thinking and tomfoolery, could have been the end of me. I am happy to say that, by the grace of God, I live.

1. San Gabriel Mountains

Having attended an environmental gathering in Los Angeles, I decided to explore the San Gabriel mountain ranges northeast of the city. I was driving a large, rear-wheel drive, Lincoln rental car. It was what I had, not recognizing the fact that a four-wheel drive vehicle would be needed where I was going.

I drove on a good four-lane highway for some distance north of the metropolitan area. I could see the mountains to the east. With the city far behind me, I turned onto a paved two-lane road leading across a wide valley, toward the mountains.

I continued to drive for about an hour before the road began to twist and turn as I ascended to higher elevations. Switchbacks soon became commonplace and I could see the valley far below. The road narrowed. I saw an unpaved road that seemed to navigate a ridgeline to the top of one of the highest mountains.

It was at this point that common sense should say, "No! Don't turn!" But I was a man on an adventure. I turned onto the unpaved road, which turned out to be a mixture of gravel and hardpan dirt. Up and up I went. The long hood of the car pointed markedly skyward. With no place to backup or turn around, I continued upward into low-hanging clouds.

I soon found myself in a very large rental car, on a primitive dirt path, high in a mountainous wilderness area. The road, now single lane, was filled with potholes and crevices. The sun was sinking over a low range of hills to the west. Why did I ever do this? I began to tremble with the realization that I may not find a way out, even if I had all the daylight in the world.

As I turned upward around a sharp curve, the car began to slide. A vertical rock cliff was on my left. A vertical drop off was on my right. And, the car was not sliding toward the cliff. I gunned the engine, spun the tires, and continued toward the mountaintop. In my head, a crescendo of voices seemed to be saying, "Stop the car and get out!" I continued on.

After the curve, the "goat path" led steeply in a straight line toward the summit. This time, there was no protection of a rock face. Extremely precipitous drop offs were on both sides of the car. I inched the car upward. At that moment, the car began to slide toward the brink. With locked brakes, it was carried on small gravel pebbles on the way to its demise, and mine.

It was at this point that I prayed. I probably should have done that before taking the unpaved road! How I longed to be back in my motel room.

The car stopped sliding and rested at an angle at the edge of the road. I gingerly turned the engine off, put the transmission in park, set the parking brake, and eased out of the car. I couldn't believe my predicament. Standing beside the car, I teetered in fear as I looked straight down into the deep gorge below.

I was safe. Now what? Twilight never felt so enjoyable. At least it was not pitch dark. I prayed, "Dear God, I got myself up here. Please get me out." In my head, a soft, calm, trusting voice said, "Back up parallel to the edge of the road and wait." I thought, "Wow! Did this mean I might die?"

I got back into the car, started the engine, and put the car into neutral. By steering only so slightly, I let gravity bring the entire huge car next to the edge.

Leaving the car running, I got out again. Okay, I did it and that's the end of that, I said to myself.

Now the voice said, "Be brave." Obviously, this was an indication of what was to come. At this point, I was willing to walk all night down the mountain and pay whatever it cost to get the car down. Should I trust this subtle inner voice? Should I continue with this lunacy? "So far, so good," I said to myself, "Why not?" If worse came to worst, I could always try to jump out at the last second!

He said, "Edge the right front wheel over the rim of the gorge and aim the rear of the car toward the other side." "Sure", I said. "Will You lift it up?" I received no answer.

I did what I was told. Using the gravity trick, I now had the car crossways on the narrow ridge. "Do I continue?" No answer. The voice hadn't failed me yet. God had clearly shown me the way.

Without moving, I turned the front wheels all the way to the right, facing downhill. If I continued, the left front wheel would be over the edge. It was on my side. So much for my jumping out "Plan B", I couldn't jump out.

I held my breath, leaned over the passenger side, and let gravity carry me downward onto the slender ridgeline. The left wheel careened into space, but the right wheel held. I was now safe, although pointing steeply downhill. Slowly, I edged my way down the mountain, shaking all the way.

When I got back to the four-lane highway, I stopped at a diner for coffee. The coffee did not have a calming effect, but I was out of the car. I finally arrived back at my hotel room, well after midnight. I fell in bed thanking God for my salvation. I also pledged to never again take such a large rental car into obvious danger.

2. Allegheny Mountains

Some people never learn. This time I was in my small, front-wheel drive, Plymouth Horizon. It was mid-winter and there was snow on the ground. In addition, the region had just received a heavy ice storm. I was on my way to take a mineral-laden salt block to the family's vacation property, located high on a mountain ridge.

The vacation property was on four undeveloped acres. Deer, turkeys, bears, and bobcats crisscrossed the property. It was an ideal location for building a cabin we could use as a mountain getaway.

The trip from our home near Dulles Airport in northern Virginia to the West Virginia property took about three hours. I thought about taking one of my son's with me, but Saturday morning cartoons took priority. Making my way to West Virginia, I thought, "Why am I doing this?" It was an adventure.

Although slippery in places, the trip was relatively easy, partly due to the fact that not many other drivers were venturing onto the highways. Arriving in the valley of Lost Creek, I turned onto the dirt road that led up to the ridge area. The road was slightly wider than one lane—sound déjà vu? I didn't even think about it.

The mountain development was situated on the side of a long, steep ridge. The slope rose from about one thousand feet to three thousand feet in elevation. Properties were accessible by means of terraced lanes, level with the mountaintop. Vertical side roads on each side of the ridge served as connectors to these roads. All of the roads were unpaved.

I began my ascent onto one of the vertical roads. At the bottom, round gravel rocks were frozen to the compacted dirt of the road. This seemed, at first, to provide solid traction. Crawling steadily upward, I felt the car begin to lose its grip. I was more than halfway up my access lane. Surely I can pull my way up the rest of the way with my front wheel drive.

My prediction was wrong. The car began to slide backward down the mountain. With an ever faster gain in speed, I thought that I was doomed. I expected the car to swerve out of control and tumble downhill.

Time to pray? "Definitely, yes," I said to myself. "Please God, help me now!" He of course, had heard this plea before. The car was now out of control. I turned around in my seat and actually drove the car backward. The car was gaining speed as I drove it in reverse down the mountain. If there was going to be a crash, at least it was going to be a controlled crash.

Thank God, the car was no longer sliding backward on its own. I was now in charge of that. I must have slipped about 500 feet down the steep road. It was a bloodcurdling experience; one I never want to revisit. Finally, the car gained stability as I hit the frozen gravel—the same gravel from which I had begun my ascent.

I was able to stop the car and take inventory of my wits. "Never, never will I do this again," I promised myself. I also think God had heard that before. I turned around and left the mountain with a feeling of victory in defeat. Heading home, I pledged never again to take such a small car into obvious danger.

3. Survival beyond Luck – Valdez, Alaska

Valdez, Alaska, lies at the bottom of a natural bowl, enclosed by high mountains. To land or take off in a fixed-wing aircraft, one must fly in a spiral pattern. Taking off, it's up and up. Upon landing, it's down and down. It is a hair-raising experience.

One day, as part of a fact-finding trip in support of the Alaskan Gas Transportation Decision, I flew in a small helicopter out of Valdez to inspect a potential pipeline route that would avoid interference with a glacier. After taking off and circling many times, we reached an altitude high enough to fly over the nearby mountains. I thought that this was the scariest part of the trip. I was wrong.

As we flew high over a jagged glacier full of deep fissures, the helicopter began to shake. The experienced pilot (unskillful Alaskan pilots do not exist) immediately knew the problem. The rotors were icing up. We began to plummet. My pilot's demeanor was laid back. It was either we survive or not, but so far so good.

The pilot's intention was to let the helicopter lower itself in elevation to where warm air from the Japanese current would melt the ice. "Isn't this an awfully passive way to deal with our predicament?" I wondered. I began to pray. I found myself praying, not only for my own protection, but also for the pilot, our families, and for those people and resources that might be affected by the proposed transportation system.

Down and down we went. The helicopter began to vibrate as we started a slow descent—which soon became a fast descent. When riding in a helicopter, one has a secure feeling of being suspended by an umbrella filled with a burst of air from beneath. However, our umbrella was broken.

Where the glacier entered the ocean, I could see a large, unidentifiable whale and smaller, white Beluga whales. The panorama was stunning. I momentarily forgot we were plunging to our death. At the last moment, the helicopter seemed to leap upward as ice spun off of the rotors. We were safe. I thanked God for his help. I think He receives a lot of "thank you" prayers from Alaskan pilots.

Palms On the Table

Some moments in life can be quite sobering. Sometimes these moments come right out of the blue, when we least expect it. My moment occurred at an innocuous banquet, one of many I attended as part of my professional career.

I remember being bored as I sat at the table, messing around with a fork, as the speaker gave his speech. I glanced at a palm frond placed on the table as a decoration. The frond was soaked with wine.

Suddenly, a whole host of pent up feelings overwhelmed me. I thought of Palm Sunday, sacrificial wine, and guilt. Were we crucifying Christ in our irreverent use of palm branches?

Why do such feelings erupt all of a sudden? Do we carry guilt with us all of the time? What did this moment mean to me? Did I purposely leave Christ absent from my life? The abrupt awareness of these feelings caused me to jot down the following prose on one of the dinner napkins.

Palms in Tennessee

I saw some palms today.

Actually, they were leaves or fronds lying on tables,
    tables of a banquet, social hour in the parlance,
    at a business meeting.

Plates, glasses, liqueur, hors d'oeuvres, and spilt wine
    covered the palms.

"A nice touch to the décor," said one of the palms.
"Yes, I'm sure they have many," said another.

When I was young, palms were precious.
I would care for them, carefully weaving them
   into crucifixes, the signs of my Christ.

Palms and Palm Sunday, penance and forgiving and caring,
   they all had meaning.
And now, these palms are a rude awakening.

Strange, how palms have meaning.
For September in Tennessee and a long way from home,
   these palms have meaning.

For what do they mean? I'm not quite sure.
Is it death or reality or life ... or hope?

Maybe it's more of meaning itself,
   of caring for more important things than spilt wine.

Somehow, I feel the meaning,
    I must care for my palms again.

I must learn to care, and to love,
    and to believe.

My palms and I, maybe we will not meet again,
    not in another place and not in another time,
    lest death.

(Upon glancing at a banquet table, 1979)

Passing It On

In our wake, we leave behind many products of our endeavors. For good or bad, we affect many lives, some directly and others indirectly. Too rarely do we hear direct feedback on the positive impact we made along the way. The following are snippets of some positive feedback I've been blessed to hear, a result of putting God's will into practice.

1. University Students

I have always tried to motivate students and give them a sense of wonder about the world around us. At the end of each semester, I would receive "thank you" notes from many of my students.

Thirty years after I left teaching at Indiana State University, my family and I passed through Terre Haute, Indiana. We stopped at the City's Nature Center. The naturalists at the Center, a husband and wife team, welcomed us with open arms. I did not know them, and they were giving us VIP treatment. Was this a case of mistaken identity?

It turns out they were former students of mine. They said that it was because of me that they dedicated their lives to educating people, children and adults, about the natural environment. My inspiration, they said, made a difference in their lives. I said, "Wow, I didn't know. Thank You."

2. Science Fair Entrants

For over 15 years, I have been judging high school science fairs, mostly at the state level. For me, its fun and I get to stay involved with science. Some students conduct their research in university labs, within the scientific context of a large, well-funded, multi-disciplinary research project. Other students conduct their scientific investigation out of poorly funded rural schools, without state-of-the-art equipment, and with very little help.

I often attempt to motivate science fair students to strive toward a professional line of work, with college training. Sometimes, I am the only one, outside of their teachers, who has shown them encouragement.

About eight years ago, I came across a promising student from rural Virginia. She was at the top of the competition, due to her ability to explain her research. Her research focused on understanding pollution sources and potential control from a watershed viewpoint. She read extensively from the background scientific literature and had a well-designed scientific method. She clearly had her act together.

Surviving competition at the local and regional levels, she had reached the state science fair since her freshman year. Now as a senior, she was awarded the State Science Fair Award for Environmental Sciences. With her award scholarship and other awards from environmental organizations, she could afford to attend almost any educational institution of higher learning.

After being advised that she had won, but before the award ceremony, I took an opportunity to speak with her. Somehow, I diverged from my normal admonishment about college for a different one. I told her there is more to life than acclaim and notoriety. I told her that she had now reached a point in her life where she had received an investment from so many sources: books, teachers, relatives, friends, and science fair judges. She had a natural ability to influence others. Now, she had a responsibility to give back to her community and to upcoming students.

The next year, I learned that she had turned down acceptance to some prominent universities, deciding to stay home where she could help some friends and relatives, and attend a local community college. In the next few years, I saw her at the state science fair where she was a special award judge for the State Water Pollution Association.

Three years ago, I found her at the International Science and Engineer Fair in Albuquerque, New Mexico. She was volunteering as staff support for the Environmental Science judges. Lacking a Ph.D., she could not be a judge, but had found a way to serve.

I learned that she spent her last two years obtaining a biology degree at William and Mary College, not far from her hometown. She has been accepted into a Ph.D. program at Virginia Tech University with a major in environmental science. Now, her volunteer job of assisting environmental sciences judges at the international fair brought the story to a full circle—teacher helps student, now student helps teacher. At subsequent fairs in Atlanta, Georgia, and Reno, I looked for her to no avail. I will try again next year.

Her mother was at the Albuquerque Fair. She took my arm and said, "I want to tell you something special. You had a tremendous influence on my daughter when you spoke to her at that state science fair. She was on a path to turning into a conceited whiz kid. She really took your words to heart. Thank You."

Sometimes, it's the little things we do and say that make the biggest difference. It has been my pleasure to reach out to students. I thank God for this gift, both in ability and opportunity.

3. Acquaintances

A few years ago, I attended our annual church retreat in mountainous Orkney Springs, Virginia. The retreat focused on how people can become empowered to live positive lives through the encouragement of others.

At the retreat, which became rather emotional at times, a middle-aged woman came up to me. She said that I had empowered her. She said, a few years back, I had said a few kind words to her. She had been in a depression and feeling worthless. I had provided her the confidence to turn her life around. She wanted to thank me.

I only vaguely remembered the earlier encounter. Without conscious effort, just giving honest words of encouragement, I had made a difference in that woman's life. Encouraging words are very powerful. We should use them freely.

4. Scouts

In high school, I was a boy scout, earning 50 merit badges. During the 1950's, I think that was some kind of record. After the Marine Corps, I served as an assistant scoutmaster, and then a scoutmaster. Later, for my preteen sons, I served as a Cub master.

As a scout leader, one can have a positive influence on children. A scout leader must be a good role model, strong in character, respected by parents, and full of trivia about life skills.

At the end of meetings, we would gather hands-over-shoulders. I would bring to mind what we had done and what lies ahead. I always ended meetings with the words, "May the Great Scoutmaster of all scouts guide us and direct us on our path. Amen." I'm not sure that these words are politically acceptable today, but I got away with it then. Such motivation instilled enthusiasm, which lasted well beyond meeting time.

Many years later, a mother of one of my former scouts met me at a grocery store. She said that her son, now in college, turned his life around as a result of my Cub Scout program. His path was leading to him hanging out with gang members and getting into drugs. Through Scouting, he found a purpose in life.

This year, a clerk at our post office told me her son (now a teacher in high school) was one of my cub scouts. His need to "give back" came from his years in scouting.

Thank God for positive youth programs. I feel blessed to be a part of one of them.

5. Low Income Elderly

After leaving government service, I wanted to change my focal point in life from the big picture to one-on-one contact with individual people. I wanted to be out of the spotlight and into lending a helping hand as anonymously as possible.

I always wanted to work with my hands, so I acquired state certification as a home repair contractor. I think that I was the only person who was a certified Senior Ecologist and also a certified Home Repair Contractor.

With this permit, I could help low income elderly people with their home repairs. I charged about half that of other contractors and did even the small jobs that were not worth the time and effort of other contractors. Thus, I could "be there" for the elderly. With the elderly, I would take my time, do a good job, help with ancillary minuscule jobs, and be a sounding board.

Spanning the repair of loose siding, leaking faucets, broken electrical switches, and corroded handrails, I would do it all. Many times, the elderly were living by themselves, as a widow or widower. Often, they did not have any children living close by or anyone who had the time to help them.

A commonality of these lonely people was that they needed to talk. They would talk about being overcharged at the store, not being able to get out, children who would not visit, sick relatives, and a multitude of other woes. From one thing to the next, they would talk over and over again about the same problems. I think that, in many cases, they just needed someone who would listen.

More than once, an elderly person would seem to be in a talking "loop," unable to stop. I would look into their eyes, sometimes holding them, and say, "its okay. You are not alone." At that moment, I would see a glint in their eyes. They would relax, with a real sense of contentment. I could actually see the peace of God come over them. Such times as these make all of life's troubles go away, both for them and for me. These moments are special.

6. The Homeless

As a home repair contractor for the poor, I was also asked to help the rich. It seems the affluent have just as hard a time finding someone to do small repair jobs as the poor. But, the rich have discretionary money to spend for their pleasure. Often, I would install various doodads just so they could have new toys to play with. Many times, I would replace new fixtures for perfectly good old ones.

While working for the rich, I would talk about the needs of the poor. Immediately, they would offer whatever was needed from their homes and replace those furnishings with new ones. This was great. Soon, I became a "legitimate" Robin Hood, bringing very high quality furniture and other household items from the rich to the poor.

Most in need of furniture were those who recently had been homeless. Social service organizations could place them in transient housing, but they would sleep on the floor in their unfurnished quarters. Homeless families needed sturdy sofas, trundle beds, full or queen-size beds, and kitchen tables. They all needed computer systems for either email or homework. As an aside, all apartments where the homeless were placed had high-speed internet access.

Suddenly, my blue pickup truck, with ladder rack and American flags on the doors, became recognizable throughout town. Over the last few years, I have transported over a hundred tons of furniture and household goods for the low-income elderly and the homeless.

It's a cruel world and most homeless individuals and families are not destitute by choice. Loss of a job and inability to pay rent can lead to eviction in a short period of time. Exorbitant medical bills can leave a family penniless and deeply in debt. Company closings, bankruptcies, seized assets, and the like can force even the "well off" to become homeless. The homeless problem is exacerbated in affluent communities where the lure of employment brings families which are unable to cope with the high cost of living. Shelters and government-rented motel rooms quickly overflow.

While interacting with the homeless, it has been my pleasure to see many success stories. One story involves a woman whose husband left her. Alone with two small children, she could not keep up the payments on her three bedroom house. The bank took the house. In the newspaper, she found a two bedroom apartment available at a low rate, but barely affordable on her waitress salary.

She never saw her absentee landlord. One day, she found a sheriff's deputy at her door asking her to leave. The building was being sold and the man to whom she had been making rent payments did not own the building. She found herself out on the streets, without a place to live and with a broken-down car. Unable to get to work, she lost her job.

For a few weeks, a county social worker placed her family in a shelter. With help, she found a job as a store clerk within walking distance from her new low income housing apartment. It was at this time that I came into the picture, lugging furniture for her unfurnished residence. After a period of time, she moved to a government subsidized townhouse nearby. While there, social workers helped her complete her nursing degree. She is now a homeowner with a nice car. This woman went from being destitute to being a home owner within a few years—quite an accomplishment.

7. Shut-Ins

Shut-ins are those who, due to illness or disability, are unable to leave their home or residence. For several years, I've had the opportunity to interact with shut-in people in my role as Lay Eucharistic Visitor for our church. Along with a partner, I bring communion in the form of consecrated bread and wine to those who were not able to attend church services. Such visits convey to shut-ins a sense that they are not alone and that they have a caring ear for their concerns.

It's always meaningful to see the effect of communion on those who receive it. The act triggers gray eyes to brighten and smiles of joy to appear. Just the visit is cause for inspiration.

At an Alzheimer ward of a nursing home, those visited will awake from a deep lethargic stupor as we join hands and say the Lord's Prayer. Smiles abound as we say the words together. A sensation of pure joy fills the room. One wonders if this is what is meant by the term "God's Kingdom on Earth."

Alligator Attack

There by the grace of God go I, or in this case, us. My wife and I loved Florida. We liked to canoe in the crystal clear, spring fed waters. This incident so changed our lives that, through fear, we will never visit Florida again.

Seven years ago, we vacationed in Florida. One place we had never visited was the upstream portion of the Santa Fe River, northwest of Gainesville. The upstream section is designated as a wilderness area, just our type of venue.

We rented a canoe and proceeded upstream. It was a clear spring day with low humidity, and no blistering heat. Our goal was to see nature at its purest.

As we paddled, we saw a number of alligators slither off the bank beside us into the murky water. First, this did not bother us, because this is normal when we navigate Florida's backwaters. Second, we noted that we could not see the gators in this river when they were underwater. The water was brownish and obscured sight of anything below an inch or two. In all of the previous streams we had negotiated, the water was crystal clear, allowing us to see alligators on the bottom.

Once or twice during our movement upstream, we bumped into small alligators, scaring them as they bolted out of our way. We saw deer and herons wading in the river shallows. We stopped along the way to collect apple snails. Only later would we realize we had been collecting the snails from the top of a very large alligator den.

We found an old sandal at this location, and commented that, "Sometimes individuals just disappear." Not telling anyone where he or she is going, they are never found. Did an alligator eat this one?

Upon leaving, my wife stepped into a large depression. Backing off, she could see, without a doubt, the imprint of a huge alligator foot.

After returning quickly to our canoe, we continued upstream. Primitive vines, palms, and dense vegetation seemed to reach out from the narrow banks. Finally, we reached very shallow water where the stream emerged as an underground stream. We turned around. Carried by the current we moved easily downstream.

My wife, Peg, was in the front of the canoe. She would paddle on one side of the canoe for a while, then paddle on the other. I was in the rear, paddling using various strokes, and steering. We were enjoying quite an ideal, leisurely adventure. We headed back through one of the most scenic parts of the river,

Peg was paddling gracefully on her left side, in proper form. Then, just as she began to lift her arm to place the paddle on her right side, a terrifying explosion of water and sound shattered the tranquility of our paradise. A twelve foot alligator shot upward from the dark water on her left side. With mouth wide open, it rose higher and higher in nanoseconds, twisting in a death spiral. It was trying to grab her left arm and drag her under the water.

By the grace of God or by happenstance, at that very moment, Peg was switching her paddle to the other side. Only because of that, the alligator had missed his mark. It rose with its underside facing Peg. I vividly remember that gaping mouth forming a wide "V." With its tail still in the water, it turned as it extended its entire trunk out of the water. Then, it began to fall toward me. I was afraid that it would catch one of its legs on the side of the canoe and tip us over as it began to slide back into the water. I thought of the most horrible outcome of this unfolding disaster.

As the alligator continued to twist and fall, its back pushed against the canoe. I felt a rush of air and water spray as it fell back into its dark hideaway. We were safe. Despite the fact that I can give an account of the entire attack, it all occurred within two or three seconds, though it seemed like an eternity.

As soon as the water exploded, Peg knew something was not right. She leaned to her right, away from the sound. It was at this point that I thought the canoe would tip over and feared both of us would end up in the alligator's lair. My role was to remain calm and keep the canoe as stable and upright as I could. It worked. Peg didn't say a thing. Silence is golden.

With the alligator back in the water, I continued paddling downstream. With the paddle across her knees, Peg sat motionless. With the current in our favor, my steady but hurried paddling quickly carried us downstream away from the site of our near demise.

While we moved further and further down and out of the wilderness area, I began to have a strange feeling. The back of the canoe seemed to quiver. It actually was vibrating incredibly fast, like a tuning fork. I realized that Peg, apparently sitting motionless up front, was actually shaking rapidly. Her trembling was causing the back of the canoe to quiver.

As I explained how the back of the canoe was vibrating and even sculling us through the water, I said to her, "Well, I've heard of shiver me timbers, but I've never heard of shiver me canoe." She was not impressed. Her reply was, "I'm alright. I'm just sitting here." Later, she realized that she also had been holding her breath so long she feared she was having a heart attack. Her chest hurt for days after the incident.

We got back to the unattended dock where we stowed the canoe, and departed. We did not talk much about the near mishap, preferring to put it behind us. As it turns out, we should have dwelt on our near-fatal outcome a little bit longer, because the next day, we went to the Suwannee River. The Suwannee River is a large black water river, not one to explore in a canoe. So we went to Manatee Springs to see manatees. The Manatee Springs flow into the Suwannee.

We rented another canoe. With a round bottom, this canoe was not very stable. I figured it would be just fine for the placid waters surrounding the

"Springs." We paddled through a small area near the dock and then decided to venture out into the open water of the Suwannee where manatees also could be seen.

Very soon, we were teetering as our canoe attempted to remain upright in the waves and wake of large boats. We saw a fish jump out of the water beside us and land several yards away. I mentioned to Peg that this was an "avoidance technique" fish used to escape from large predators. "What large predators lurk in these waters?" I wondered. The question did not need answering. We immediately headed for shore.

Near shore, we ventured into a narrow channel formed by an island and the riverbank. On the island, we saw alligator dens and large footprints. We thought of that sandal that we found on our trip into the wilderness. In our wobbly canoe, we quickly paddled our way back to the safety of Manatee Springs.

Were there lessons learned on this Florida vacation? Yes. We learned to think first before we undertook a potentially perilous adventure. Second, we learned that life is very fragile and fleeting. Within an instant, our life together could have been turned upside down, literally.

Was it really by chance that Peg switched sides at the last split second? I don't think so. I feel that the entire incident was a reminder of how much Peg and I have. We have been blessed with happiness and love that few share. We have not forgotten our lesson.

A Daughter is Drowning

Yes, life can change in an instant. One moment it is peaceful and quiet. The next moment it can be horrific. Such a life altering moment came to my family on a summer outing. The feeling that it leaves behind never goes away.

We were in an electric powered row boat on one of our favorite lakes in northern Virginia. It was a warm, calm, and sunny day—ideal for a family outing. My wife Peg, her daughters ages twelve and fourteen, and I were about a half mile from shore. Peg and her oldest daughter chose to go swimming. They lowered themselves off the side of the boat as we sat at anchor. They horsed around, splashing water on us in the boat. A good time was being had by all.

Peg was swimming behind the boat. She was a natural swimmer and, as a youth, she had been a lifeguard. Her daughters had been on a swim team since entering school, and were good swimmers. I could not swim, but I could tread water pretty well. Peg was on her back in the water, about twenty feet away. I said to the twelve year old, "Where is your sister?" We looked near the boat. Then, we scanned far out into the water all around us. She was not to be found.

Fear struck me instantly. Heavy breathing paced with the thumping of my heart. "No, this cannot happen!" I could not believe she was missing. I would not accept that she had drowned. I yelled to my wife to look out for her. I was at a loss over what to do. Somehow, I knew that staying put was the best course of action. Seconds seemed like minutes.

Near the bow of the boat, I heard the splash of water. I saw it spurt upward as a hand appeared out of the water. I lunged forward and grabbed the hand at the wrist. I was not going to let go. I shouted to Peg, "Come help, she's drowning!" I held on for dear life. I now held her wrist with both hands. She seemed so heavy. I lifted with all of my strength.

The boat was tipping over, motivating the younger daughter to help balance the boat. Peg was nearing the front of the boat when I lifted her head above the waterline. I was ecstatic. My joy was short lived as I realized that I could not hold her weight much longer.

Peg dove under the water. She seemed to be gone forever. I thought, "Now, have I lost her?" Then, she popped out of the water holding the anchor line. She said that it was wrapped around her daughter's ankle. She dove in again. This time, I felt more at ease. But, I was beginning to literally lose my grip.

All at once, the drowning daughter's weight seemed to be lost as she popped up in the water, screaming to be pulled into the boat. This, I knew was a good sign. She was breathing and complaining, "I want in the boat! I want in the boat!" And coincidentally, Peg was back on the surface.

While under water she had tried to lift the concrete anchor with its line wrapped around her ankle. Unintentionally, the rope had wrapped itself tight, binding her legs as she fought to lift herself and the anchor to the surface. With Peg and both daughters in the boat, I said, "Now we are safe." I lifted the anchor and started toward the dock. Everyone was emotionally spent.

How long does it take to pray? How many words make a prayer? Did I have time to ask God for help? Did anyone else take time to ask for Divine aid? Yes, I know that I prayed while going through the actions of grabbing an emergent hand. I know my daughter prayed, because she said so. And, I know Peg pleaded with the Almighty for help when all seemed lost. Prayers can be brief or long. It's the meaning that counts.

Church on the Prairie

For the last eight summers, Peg and I have traveled to a small prairie farm in northwestern Montana. We spend two weeks with Peg's sister and brother-in-law. It offers us a clean break from the hustle and bustle of Northern Virginia. The land lacks the dreadful humidity of the east, but makes up for it by the searing heat of the big sky, high plains.

The farm is a "hobby farm," with chickens, ducks, and other fowl. Its owners are teachers at a high school in a small town, fourteen miles to the south. It is a great area to fish and contemplate. It is also a long way from a church of choice. Given the distance, the cost of fuel and time, most worship is done in the home.

I know that God is everywhere and one doesn't need to be in a conventional house of worship to experience God. Bibles, songbooks, and the heart, are mobile. It is what one does with them that is important.

For two Sundays of each summer, the four of us hold a 45-minute, informal service in the home. We call it, "doing Church." Unleavened bread and grape juice serve as the sacramental last supper offerings, accompanied with enduring hymns, Bible readings, and prayers.

Large church services certainly can be inspirational and uplifting. The structured liturgy can be comforting, with its traditional uniformity and consistency. But, at the same time, one person tends to lead and congregants tend to follow — more spectators than participants.

At the home church service, everyone participates in an integrated offering of love and homage to God. There are no strong leaders or followers. The Bible tells us, "...where two or three come together in my name (Jesus), there am I with them." (Matthew 18:20)

With mountain vistas in view, birds singing, and waves of grain as a backdrop, when we do Church on the prairie, it is very meaningful. Sometimes, when we are back at home ensnarled in the multitude activities of a busy traditional church, I reflect on the simplicity of doing Church on the prairie.

Neighbors Can Be Everlasting Friends

By now, I have known many people who have died: my brother, my parents, friends, and acquaintances. I am not afraid of dying, so it follows that I am not bothered when I think of them. I remember them as individuals with special attributes and particularities.

Recently, I have been thinking of my neighbors a few doors away. They are a brother and sister trying to make a go of it in this world. The brother recently married and has moved to southern Virginia. The sister still lives in the house, leased from a very nice entrepreneurial couple. She plans to move in about a year to devote her talents to being a full time missionary.

One summer, their mother came to visit and stayed while undergoing cancer treatments. The treatments were not successful and she died. I talked to her on an occasional basis. She was friendly and quite frank about her prognosis. All I could do was be a supportive friend. I think she appreciated the consideration.

About a year after her death, her estranged husband came to visit and stayed. He was very friendly, always saying hello and looking me up to discuss my activities. I think he did some light plumbing work. After not seeing him for some time, I asked his daughter where he was. It seems he had died unexpectedly, from a stroke.

Both husband and wife were separated in life's maelstrom. Each was a human being with wishes and worries and kind words to say. I am glad for their children that there is someone they know locally who has shared knowledge of their parents. I don't know how their parents felt regarding living their lives to the fullest. I remember neither one of them expressed regret.

They bring to mind that people do live a complete life cycle from birth to old age. Lucky are we who move through infancy to survive life's adventures. In the end, we drift back toward the simplicity of early years. Such contemplation led me to write the following words.

My block my world

When I was young,
    So very, very young,
    The world was my crib,
    my bed.

Soon, I thought the world was as large as from the top of the
    kitchen table to the top of the great high-backed chair.

Before long, I knew the whole house,
> it was so large.

When I was four years old,
> I was proud of myself for knowing my whole block ...
> from one end to the other.

I could not get lost.
I could run and play in its entire length.

By seven, I knew my neighborhood and traveled far.

When fourteen, I could tour the entire town,
> every street,
> every house.

I even took a trip out of the State.

By twenty-five, I had traveled far and wide.
Since then, I have felt free to roam the world.

But, lately, I have noticed a difference.
It has been a year since I have driven outside of town,
    a month since my last car ride.

I remember, only last week,
    I walked the entire length of my block,
    perhaps for the last time.

Now, I lay in my bed, and …
    my world seems so small,
    so very, very small.

(Upon seeing an old man leaning on a cane at the end of a block, 1977)

Singing

It is said that singing is the best way to heaven, especially if you sing hymns. If this is the case, those of us in our church's Front Porch Singers group have it made in the shade. Mostly, we sing old time gospel songs to residents of nursing homes, assisted living centers, and subsidized low-income housing.

I have had a problem with singing, and still do. The problem is that I can't sing, at least not on key or in harmony. This trait is considered to be poor form for a singer. But, I look good.

I bring maracas for the folks to use as percussion instruments. The residents participate by shaking them to the beat of the music. I kid around a lot using my train hat and whistle and washboard. Being able to play only a few self-taught chords, I consider myself a backup guitarist. However, I do play those chords well, and loud.

When I was ten years old, my father would let me accompany him on car trips from our home in Chicago to our newly purchased farm in southern Indiana. Along the way, he taught me to sing "Clementine," an old western song about a miner and his daughter. We developed a close relationship during our singing sessions on those long trips.

When my first set of children were old enough, I bought a guitar and began to teach them some old songs. As they grew older, they finally broke the news to me that I was no singer. In fact, my singing voice was repulsive. I put away my guitar and never sang again until my second set of children also was old enough to sing with me. I got out my guitar. Their response was even more depressing. Again, I packed my guitar. My depression concerning being able to sing was compounded by the fact that I like to sing.

Several years ago, our church began to create a new singing ministry to serve shut-ins. Being unable to keep silent, I said that I had a guitar. Of course, that was all that was needed. I joined the group with the understanding that I would not play as a lead guitarist or singer. That was fine, all are welcome. Right away, we began to sing simple ditties, including "Clementine."

We have been playing together for about eight years. I am one of the mainstays. It has brought hope and inspiration to many people who thought that they would never again hear those old gospel songs. And, it has bolstered our faith and compassion for others.

There are many heartening stories of feedback from devotees. I'll share one about a husband and wife who lived in an assisted living center. He was the pastor of a church for over sixty years. She was always by his side. They had fallen into despair, feeling that the world to which they had given all of their energy had moved on, leaving them by the wayside. Our visits gave them a new spark and a reason for living. He joined us up front as we sang the old hymns.

Singing is good for the soul. Why didn't I get rid of that old guitar? Why did I make myself so vulnerable by opening up about my ownership of a guitar? God does indeed work in mysterious ways.

Traveling

Travelers share a lot in common, namely boredom. Flying to a far flung business destination and back can drain energy, creating dreary-eyed people everywhere. Whether commuting, on a long airplane flight, or in meetings, I get bored stiff. It's not long before I become lost in thought about peculiar people or situations I view in momentary glimpses.

When traveling, loneliness is unavoidable and communing with God is almost inevitable. The long hours take their toll. One becomes connected to fellow travelers. Often, one wonders what individual travelers are thinking about themselves, God, and their companions. The following are examples of my drifting thoughts on the road.

Glance at thirty-nine thousand feet

Maybe she likes wine.
    I do not know.

She appears chic,
    as she holds her plastic cup,
half standing by her seat.

Is it for show
    or just a casual gesture?

Airplane wine was never my favorite.
    Neither wine nor cup seems appropriate or appealing.

Coffee or Cola,
> not Chablis or Burgundy,
> will get me by.

She will pass through the night, and
> I will write my lines,
> as we wait the dawn.

(Returning aboard the redeye special, 1985)

Over Kansas passing time

A five hour flight,
> just a hop, I thought.

One reads or works or sleeps,
> but none are mine to do.

Others read their thick books,
> sum their tallies, and sleep.

The plane drones on,
    a good time to think,
    as the past and future are caught in time.

In time, we'll be there,
    thousands of miles from where we've been,
    to return thousands of miles back again.

We pass back and forth,
    doing and undoing,
    escaping and finding,
    And returning again.

(Returning aboard the redeye special, 1985)

One learns a lot when driving to work. Traveling long distances to work takes time. Commuting a short distance in urban traffic takes a very long time. Near Washington, DC, it seems every hour is a rush hour. At peak commuting hours, it can take an hour to go ten miles.

A driver has few options to eliminate boredom. One can listen to the radio or compact disc, but after a year it becomes background noise. A recorded book offers some relief; however, there are only so many books one likes to hear. Recently, cellular phones have become the anticipated relief. I only had one accident as the result of using one while driving.

Inevitably, a commuter's mind drifts into senseless thought. For some, commuting can provide time to think of solutions to workplace or life's problems. It is said that idleness is the devil's playground. Such time can become dangerous for bosses, colleagues, and husbands or wives.

For me, commuting became a time to be pensive. Why are trees only so tall? Why are mountains not higher? Why aren't roads wider? Why do people with the most expensive cars go the slowest?

One time, on the way to work, I glanced out the passenger side window and saw a middle-aged man standing with a shovel. He was looking at a small field. A teenage girl stood beside him. A small boy played in the field. My mind drifted toward possibilities. Later that day, I wrote the following prose.

Clearing the field

It's a small field,
> not much of a plot.

My father, brother, and I,
> we look at it on this cold April morning.

The crows are calling
> and it feels almost like autumn.

People pass on the road and watch us,
> as we hold onto our world.

No hurry, while we take our time,
> just clearing today.

Somehow, I feel close to Dad
    and understand his feeling,
    of being complete, I think.

And mine is much more than being his little girl,
    more as a daughter who understands.

So, like father and son, we stand together
    and survey our world, as mom fixes lunch.

It's a good feeling, almost warm.
    Yet somehow, I feel it won't return.

But for today, we are just clearing the field.

(Thoughts while passing by in another world, 1986)

Over a decade later, I found myself still commuting on that same road. I looked for the field, and found it unrecognizable. Sadness easily crept into my feelings. That field and that moment shared so many years ago was gone. That evening, with a sad heart, I wrote the following.

Clearing the field, addendum

The survey stakes mark the lines,
    as the road widening project begins.

Your house is now boarded and closed forever,
    and your field lays barren, waiting for the blade.

Do you remember not long ago when you stood here?
    Are your memories blurred by your adult years?

I wonder where you are and what you hold dear.
    I often think of that day and that moment in time.

Have you held it close to your heart? Was it as
    fleeting and ephemeral as this old road?

Now as I pass by, I also only have the memory.
>   Will I be left to keep the ember glowing?

I wish you the memory of what I realized.
>   May you hold it close to your heart.

(Thoughts while passing by in the same world, 1999)

One bit of prose is especially poignant. It is probably typical of a journey of many commuters who pass the same intersection day in and day out.

Commuter friend

I see you again,
>   standing by the road.

Each day you keep your vigil,
>   watching and waiting.

Nine, ten, and eleven you have been,
    and every morning I have seen you,
    looking in each car as you wait for school.

Is it your father you seek?
    Or, are you curious or bored?

You have become my friend.
    Your smile, anticipation, and concern,
    have become my own.

Someday, I will pass his way again,
    and you will not be here.

I will not feel sorry or glad,
    for I will understand,
    my friend.

(While repetitively commuting, 1984)

The Great Adventure

I started to write this story as a diary. I did not know where it would lead. I still don't know for sure how it will end. Maybe it just goes on and on. It is a story that many families have shared in one form or another. It usually begins with the same words, "it's malignant cancer." What often follows are all of the hard-hitting emotions: denial, courage, helplessness, and love. Usually, God creeps into the story at some point. Sometimes, He is met with anger, often with resolute love. This is our story.

Wednesday, April 16, 2008

Yesterday, as we sat with the doctor, he said, "You will die with this, if not from it." It was tax day. "Death and Taxes", how ironic. He is a specialist's specialist, dedicated to thoracic surgery on lung cancer using minimally invasive surgery. An oncologist referred us to him the day before.

We never thought that we would face the big "C." That happened to other people. Now, my wife Peg has one of her several lung spots diagnosed as "Bronchoalveolar carcinoma (BAC)," a non-small cell cancer variation of "adno-carcinoma." Following a biopsy, our HMO pulmonary specialist gave the news to us on April 1st. It came in the form of an evening phone call to our home. When he called, our family surrounded Peg.

The biopsy itself was out of the ordinary. The biopsy needle severed an artery in the lung and she lost over a quart of blood, with more in her lung. A simple in-and-out biopsy, turned into a 24-hour hospital stay.

How fast events happen. She is to have a chemical stress test, a special lung capacity test, blood work, and a checkup before her surgery, a week from Friday. This may be one of two surgeries over the next few weeks, followed by "harsh chemotherapy." The chemotherapy is adjuvant chemotherapy, which is used to treat rogue cells and small fast growing cell clusters that are released and settle elsewhere as a result of the surgery.

Peg's PET scan did not show any "hot" areas outside of the lungs. This is good. The BAC has not visibly metastasized. The surgeon's knowledge and experience (over two hundred such surgeries) has led him to believe that BAC tends to spread within the lung. Since more "spots" may appear and enlarge, Peg may be meeting with the surgeon for the rest of her life (good thing he is young).

Tumors like BAC tend to grow slowly. This is good and bad. Fast growing tumors would be life threatening within a short period of time. And, since they absorb chemicals rapidly, chemotherapy and radiation has a good chance of killing the cancer. Slow growing nodules allow time to "deal" with the disease, but are not very responsive to the short time frame of radiation and chemotherapy.

Thursday, April 17, 2008

It has started. This morning, Peg had a preoperational blood test. This noon, our two-and-a-half year old grandson Austin, and I will meet Peg for lunch. She will have gone to our HMO to pick up a 2005 CT scan of her lung. Austin and I will take it to the surgeon who will compare it to the most recent scan.

Apparent growth in her lung nodules may be an artifact due to the way a CT scan "slices" them, since they are not round. However, the measured growth in the largest nodule is too much to be explained away. He just wants to see for himself.

We wonder how we ever got into this mess. Peg has never smoked. It may be due to exposure to secondhand smoke, Bromine inhalation in a college lab, radon exposure in her childhood basement bedroom, or who knows what. The fact is that she has BAC.

Now, we are resigned to fight the disease. Routine monitoring and God's Grace, repeated surgery and chemotherapy, coupled with slow growing tumors, should allow Peg to have a long life.

Friday, April 18, 2008

Calmness came over us a few days ago. I wonder if my grandson Austin helped. I take care of Austin and his older brother Ian while his mother and father work.

The two of us were riding in my pickup one day when Austin asked, "What's wrong?" It was quite a perspective for a two-and-a-half year old. I said, "Papa and Momma need your help." He said, "What?" I said to Austin, "We need you to tell Jesus that we need Him." He has never been connected with Jesus as much as Ian was at his age. Nevertheless, I knew he was in touch.

Tears came to Austin's eyes as he sat motionless for about two minutes. Then, he turned to me and said, "I don't have a telephone." I left the subject. Two days later, I asked Austin if he had talked to Jesus. He said, "Yes." Then laughing, he said, "I didn't need a telephone." A toddler had tricked me.

Friday, April 25, 2008

Peg is in surgery. She aced all of her pre-surgery tests. The doctor said everything is a go for a bronchoscopy to have a look in the trachea and bronchi and laparoscopic surgery to remove one or two tumors in her right lung.

We arrived at the hospital at 5:30 a.m. She went into surgery at 7:15 a.m. We held hands and frequently kissed as she was prepared for surgery. She looked so pretty and relaxed. I should hear something from the doctor around 9:15 a.m.

It is now 10:30 a.m. and I am really anxious. Susan, administrative aide to Peg's hand surgeon, and a member of our church, surprised me in the waiting room. She came to sit with me. She has waited with me for three hours.

When I was called in to see the doctor at 10:45 a.m., Susan went with me. The doctor found a cancerous lesion in her upper lobe that was not seen by the oncologist or radiologist. The doctor removed cancerous lesions in the upper two lobes of her right lung. No lobes were removed, only wedges. Another area in the lower lobe was removed, but it was not cancerous. The surgeon is thinking about leaving one spot in her left lung for now, using it as a benchmark for its growth and detection of other spots, should they develop.

Next is intensive chemotherapy, followed by removal of cancer from her left lung. Then, another round of chemotherapy is reasonable. What all this means is that Peg should have a long life. Monitoring will be needed and further surgery or chemotherapy treatment, if needed.

It is now 11:30 a.m. Peg is in the Intensive Care Unit (ICU) where she will stay overnight. I have not seen her yet. They are supposed to get her up and walking to avoid pneumonia. She may come home tomorrow (Saturday) or the next day.

It is 1:00 p.m. and I am with Peg in the intensive care unit. She is in a great deal of pain and very drowsy. Her blood pressure is very low as is as her blood oxygen level. She is in no condition to walk.

I found a finger swollen on her right arm where an oxygen sensor was placed. Her right arm cannot have any pressure cups, IVs, or shots because her hand's lymph system has been destroyed by radiation to treat a persistent diffuse giant cell tumor in her wrist. I had them move the sensor to one of her toes.

Now, at 4:40 p.m., her status is unchanged. The doctor has just arrived to see her. She barely awoke to talk to him. He commented on how sensitive she is to anesthesia and painkillers.

At separate times, two clergy came from our church and prayed with us. Peg did not notice them.

By 6 p.m., we thought she would be in second stage recovery; she wasn't. Peg has been put on a ventilator for at least two hours in order to balance her blood gasses. Her blood has become acidic due to high carbon dioxide levels. She has been given a chemical to counterbalance all painkillers in her blood stream. These narcotics and lingering effects to the anesthesia have caused her to sleep constantly and to breathe shallow and slowly. Soon, she should wake up in a lot of pain.

By now, I'm getting pretty tired. I was looking forward to Peg being in a recovery room for the night, where she could sleep. Then, I would go home to crash. Such seems not to be the case. The problem is that she won't wake up. I'll be with her for at least another three to four hours before I consider going home for the night.

Know what? My darling is going to be okay. She will be going through some very difficult times with recovery, harsh chemotherapy, more surgery, and more chemotherapy. But, we have each other and I will be by her side all the way.

Now that she is on the ventilator, her nurse tells me that she'll likely be in ICU overnight. I think that I'll stay until about 10 p.m. and come back about 9 a.m. Each hour takes us further away from the trauma of the surgery.

This whole story started in 2000 when she went to a doctor about a growth on her right hand. Thinking it was a ganglion cyst, a surgeon tried to drain it with a syringe. It didn't drain, causing a lot of pain. A subsequent MRI determined that it was a benign diffuse giant cell tumor. Then, exploratory surgery indicated that it was throughout her wrist.

In the first major surgery, two hand surgeons worked on the hand and removed all they could. Over subsequent years five major surgeries fought the recurring tumor with no avail. Last year, Peg received twenty-nine radiation treatments on the hand. Now, the cancer driven PET scan has shown nothing growing in her wrist.

Since giant cell tumors may migrate to the lungs and become cancerous, CT scans (alternating every six months with MRI scans) were taken to find any lung spots. Very small spots were found and tracked for a few years. The spots did not appear to grow—a relief. Now those CT scans have proven to be invaluable for comparison with today's BAC lesions.

It is now 7 p.m., twelve hours after the beginning of surgery. Peg is still on the ventilator. She has been given another shot of the chemical to reverse the effects of the painkillers. She has yet to wake up. Another blood-gas blood sample will be taken. Peg may certainly stay in this intensive care unit all night.

I've been told that I will be thrown out of intensive care soon. Family members are not allowed to stay longer. However, I will be allowed to stay until Peg's replacement nurse comes aboard and the results of the blood-gas sample come in.

Saturday, April 26, 2008

I came at 8:30 a.m. and found Peg in second stage recovery. She was transferred late the previous night. She looks much better and is off the ventilator.

We have talked and walked around the recovery area two times. She has to walk four more times before she can go home.

It is 11:45 a.m. and Peg is resting. As I write this, I am looking out of the window at a courtyard below. I see family members holding and consoling a woman. Has her husband or child died? We are in a cardiovascular wing of this large hospital. Life reprieves and deaths must be the norm. I look at Peg and thank God for good surgeons and staff.

Peg is still resting. I know that she wants to go home. I must get her up soon and take her for another walk. A family friend has come to sit with us.

As I started to get Peg up, her surgeon walked in. He thinks that she is recovering well. The two post surgery lung x-rays looked good. She has a choice of removing her lung drainage tube and going home or staying another day. Peg wants to go home. The doctor wants her to do two more rounds of walking. Peg is now off for another round. We see the surgeon again in two weeks.

"Stop!" her doctor just said. Her blood oxygen level is still low. She is to do some machine-assisted breathing exercises and walk more. Should it not improve substantially, she will need to spend the night here in the hospital while the respiratory technicians work on her.

Sunday, April 27, 2008

Peg is home! We arrived home late yesterday afternoon. She is in a great deal of discomfort, but walking on an occasional basis. It looks like we will make it just fine. I expect a visit from a church lay person, bringing communion. Peg is the administrative assistant at our local Episcopal church. It is a large church so we have been inundated with questions about her status. Family members and a close friend take the brunt of most of the questions.

Thursday, May 08, 2008

Without potent painkillers, Peg has been suffering quite a lot. We have been walking outside every day. This week, she has been working three to four hours a day. Yet, after a few hours of work, she seems to hit a wall and has no energy or stamina.

Today, we met with the surgeon. He told us the results of the in-depth pathology of the tumors he removed. It seems one was BAC. The other was an adno-carcinoma. Officially, this means that she is in Stage 1 of cancer (not having spread). The bad news is that the one or more growths in her left lung may be the same as one or both of the types of cancer that were removed from her right lung.

So, now what do we do? The near-term options seem to be threefold.

Option 1. The surgeon will operate on her left lung on the 21st. She was scheduled as early as the 16th, a week from tomorrow.

Option 2. Wait to operate until the end of June. This would allow Peg more time to heal. She still can visit her sister in Montana as planned for the first part of

June. Another CT scan may shed more light on the extent and size of spots in her left lung.

Option 3. Peg would be entered into harsh chemotherapy. The second surgery would be postponed until the end of August or September, after Peg has recovered from the therapy. A CT scan could show whether the tumor(s) shrank from the chemotherapy.

Peg will discuss which way to proceed with the oncologist next Tuesday. I will not be with her. A lay chaplain and family friend will be with her. We have decided that I will still judge the International Science Fair, as planned.

Monday, June 09, 2008

It is 5:45 a.m. and we are back at our regional PET Center for another PET/CT fusion. The fusion combines biological information from Positron Emission Tomography (PET) and the anatomical information obtained from Computer Tomography

(CT) into one image. This process forms an image allowing one to see active tissue growth with precise anatomic location.

This scan was scheduled to determine if a spot in Peg's left lung has grown significantly since her last scan, two months ago. Our surgeon is also interested in following up on a hot spot on her left shoulder that showed up on her last scan. The spot may be persistent tissue inflammation from arthritis in the shoulder.

If the surgeon sees that considerable growth has occurred, he will have to operate on her left lung within a few days. If the spot has not enlarged significantly, Peg will need surgery in about a month. We longed for some normalcy in our lives, and had already planned our annual vacation to Peg's sister's farm in northwestern Montana. We would have to cancel that if she needed surgery now.

The oncologist met with us to discuss chemotherapy. The treatment will be the harshest kind. Peg is seriously wondering if it would be worthwhile.

Its potential side effects include depression, loss of hearing, kidney shutdown, inflated extremities, and a very low success rate for BAC.

Peg has extreme sensitivity to chemicals and her kidneys have shut down in two prior instances. Her lymphatic system has been destroyed in her wrist, which was radiated for giant cell cancer. She has to wear a pressure glove when flying, as any swelling would likely not go down. Is the chemotherapy worth diminishing her quality of life, given its low success rate?

Peg has been recuperating from her first lung surgery. She has been able to work full time only within the last week. Her stamina has lasted three to six hours before hitting a wall of marked exhaustion. Until recently, uncontrollable coughing has been a major problem.

Numerous people have been concerned about Peg's health. Many have inadvertently hugged her, exacerbating her discomfort. A lot of people also have asked how I have been holding up.

About two weeks ago, I went to my dentist complaining about pain in my teeth on the right side. An x-ray did not show any cavities. Upon close inspection, the dentist observed a type of abscess that is characteristic of stress. He drained the abscesses and prescribed an antibiotic. I guess Peg's illness affected me also.

Today's PET scan will last about two hours. We will obtain a duplicate of the images on a CD, which we will deliver to our surgeon on the way home. He will look at the images and call us. We are hopeful the spot has not enlarged.

Wednesday, June 11, 2008

The surgeon called today. He said that the spot in her remaining lung had not enlarged. The hot spot in her shoulder had decreased—something that cancer doesn't normally do. Her liver was hot, but that could be due to a reflection in the scan.

Bottom line, Peg gets to go to Montana! When she returns, the surgeon wants to meet with her to discuss imminent surgery and an MRI of her liver.

Monday, June 23, 2008

We are in western Montana, about fourteen miles north of a small town called Geraldine. We will stay on a small farm owned by Peg's sister and her husband. They are teachers at the town's high school. The farm is home to many chickens and other assorted small creatures. A few days ago, we butchered 87 chickens. We were very tired after that.

This is our annual summer getaway. We come here for two weeks every summer. It is tranquil and good therapy for Peg as she tends to chickens, turkeys, geese, guineas, and assorted other fowl. Peg, her sister, and brother in law seem to know each bird personally. When they are small, they all look the same to me.

We also fish for trout in reservoirs and small mountain beaver ponds. The nearby Missouri River teams with many kinds of fish. Large white pelicans soar overhead.

The land is flat, about 3,000 feet in elevation, with mountain ranges interspersed on the horizon. From the farm, the land gradually slopes down to Geraldine. The town is only visible as twinkling lights at night. It is set against the backdrop of towering Square Butte and Round Butte. The panorama reminds me of Monument Valley.

I hoped this visit would allow Peg a relaxing escape from her worries about the big "C." It hasn't, except for brief moments of gaiety or when a large crappie hits her fishing line.

When we return home, we meet with Peg's oncologist and surgeon, for tests and surgery. After recovery from the surgery, she faces four months of intense chemotherapy.

Today, a dilemma has surfaced that forces both of us to face serious choices. As background, our home situation is a bit complex. Our daughter, her husband, and their two sons live with us. In a few weeks, they will add a daughter to their family. I baby sit both boys, prepare the meals, and do everyone's laundry.

Our daughter and son-in-law plan to move to North Carolina after their daughter is born. The move is contingent upon them gaining financing for a home and finding jobs. I think that the process will extend into October or November. Peg is scheduled to begin chemotherapy in August.

Peg doesn't think that I can do all that I have been doing and also take care of her—my first priority. Something had to give, such as having our grandkids placed in expensive day care. If this happens, our daughter and son-in-law will not have enough money to move. Also, Peg thinks the kids' quality of life will be diminished by not being overseen by me. Since our daughter and son-in-law work all day, the kids and I have bonded, and I've taught them many things about nature, volunteering, and life, not available in day care. In order to keep the kids at home, Peg wants to delay chemotherapy. Thus, she is sacrificing her health and possibly her life, to keep the status quo. This is a major dilemma.

The situation is compounded further by my feelings. Since we arrived here in Montana nearly two weeks ago, I've been saying, "Guess what? I'm not baby-sitting!" I even said this when we were slaughtering and cleaning those 87 chickens on my birthday. Happy Birthday?

Babysitting had become a burden. It just wasn't as much fun as it used to be. Peg reminded me that long ago I said to her, "If I repeat something two or three times, it is a signal that I'm trying to place a high degree of importance on it." In fact, I think that is true.

My birthday comments made us realize that I'm not able to keep up with doing all of the work at home as well as my outside activities. Peg offered a short-term solution. She will fix supper every day when she comes home from work, if I will buy the food. She also will help wash, dry, and fold the clothes. She'll do this before and after surgery and into her chemotherapy, as long as she can. I think that all of us will need to sacrifice and do a little more for all of this is to work out.

Friday, June 27, 2008

This is our last full day in Montana. The sky is blue and massive as usual. It is 6 a.m. and the sky has been light for two hours. It gets dark about midnight.

Peg and I have had a great time laughing and putting our worries on the back burner. Peg caught a large shovelnose sturgeon yesterday and another the day before—a lot of caviar. Peg does quite a fish dance when she catches such a large fish.

July 1, 2008

We met with the oncologist. We had a lot of questions about: hearing loss; swelling; kidney failure; the duration of an infusion; number of infusions; how infusions are administered; need for a port implant in the chest; medicines to counteract side effects; stamina; and frequency of blood tests.

Since Peg's kidneys have shut down after surgery in the past, and since she already has some hearing loss, she has been given a different chemical treatment, one that minimizes such effects. However, numbness, tingling, a low immune response, hair loss, and joint pain are to be expected. With these new chemicals, however, she might be able to keep working. She will need to anticipate having PET scans every six to twelve months for the foreseeable future.

July 3, 2008

We have just met with the surgeon. He is really concerned about Peg's ability to recover from surgery. Following the last surgery, Peg was found to be very sensitive to chemicals, resulting in her inability to maintain adequate blood-oxygen levels. This time, he plans to use a pain pump to apply a local narcotic directly into a major nerve in her chest cavity in addition to an epidural to control pain high in her chest.

The PET scan following the last surgery shows that the tumor in Peg's left lung hasn't grown. We discussed whether to enter directly into chemotherapy or to perform the second surgery first. There are pros and cons either way. It was our call.

Peg is in favor of taking the remaining tumor out and then doing chemotherapy with both lungs surgically free of cancer. Given that chemotherapy has a low probability of treating such a tumor, we probably would end up doing surgery after chemotherapy anyway. Removing a known tumor seemed to the best course of action.

The doctor warned that he might not find the .8 cm tumor using the minimally invasive techniques used in the last surgery. In that case, he wanted permission to open up Peg's chest to reach it. Peg asked, "What would you do if it was your sister?" He said, "I would go for it." Peg said, "Well, that is your answer."

Friday, July 11, 2008

Déjà vu— I'm back in the waiting room. Susan again would show up again to keep me company. This time, its Peg's left lung. A less than .8 centimeter tumor is floating inside her left lung, away from the wall of the lower lobe. The surgeon is hoping to find and remove it using the remote control manipulation of his surgical instrument, with indirect observation of the surgical field through an endoscope. If he can't find it this way, he will spread her ribs and put his hand inside to find and remove the section of lung around the tumor.

Susan has arrived. She will wait with me until we talk to the surgeon. It's turning out to be a long wait. After three hours, I wondered if the surgeon had to open up Peg's chest. The nurse has arrived to escort us into a consultation room where we will talk to the surgeon.

The surgeon reports the operation went very well, using only minimally invasive surgery. What a relief! He says it took about an hour just to insert the epidural and the breathing tube prior to the actual surgery.

He found and removed the tumor. He also found and removed a small nodule next to it. Upon examining the lower lobe, he found a suspicious looking elongated area, which he removed. The rest of the lower lobe and the upper lobe looked fine.

The tumor and other tissues were sent to a pathologist. We will know the results in five to seven days. The amount of lung section removed should not diminish her lung capacity to any appreciable extent. She is now talking and I can see her in about a half hour.

Sunday, July 13, 2008

I spent most of yesterday with Peg, helping her wake up enough to leave the ICU. I left at 8:30 p.m., knowing that Peg was ready to be transported to the Step-Down Unit, where she would be released at some point.

Today, I have been helping her walk around the unit hallways. She needs to walk to avoid getting pneumonia. She has been on and off oxygen as we attempt to get her blood oxygen levels to a normal range. The surgeon wants her to remain in the hospital, at least through tomorrow.

It's a good thing Peg is hooked up to the pain pump and epidural. They are working fairly well. Sometimes, when I get her up to walk, her chest tube shifts and it causes her severe pain. She can take Oxycodone with Tylenol, which cuts the pain in 20-30 minutes.

There are a number of pain medications that she cannot take. This greatly limits pain control. She is allergic to codeine, which makes her break out with hives. Toradol shuts down her kidneys. Epinephrine causes an erratic heartbeat. Versad, which is used to block out memories of surgery, causes her to have nightmares that part of her life is missing. She also is allergic to the contrast dye used in CT scans.

Tuesday, August 19, 2008

Here we are again. Peg is in surgery having an implantable port placed below the skin of her upper chest. It will be attached to her vena cava, below her clavicle. Since the veins in her left arm are not accessible if her arm is swollen and IV's cannot be put in her irradiated right arm, the port is necessary for chemotherapy infusions. Once healed, needles are inserted into the port just like insulin bottles. A needle will be left in the port today because she starts chemotherapy tomorrow.

Besides meetings with doctors, blood tests and so on, we have been enjoying life since her last surgery. We spent two weeks in Montana, where Peg commiserated with chickens and fished. We immersed ourselves in family activities, including spending a lot of time with our grandchildren.

We bought a new high quality piano which plays on key (our old one could not be properly tuned). We bought a new recliner chair for our bedroom, so Peg can sit, isolated from the tumultuousness of grandkids and visitors. She can watch our new fiber-optic high digital feed of over 250 channels on our new TV.

Wednesday, August 20, 2008

We are in the oncology infusion unit. Peg has had steroids, benedryl, and other nausea reducing medicines administered orally and through her port. Now, she is receiving the first of her chemotherapy drugs, Paclitaxel. Carboplatin will follow this. Overall, we will be here about six hours.

Peg will be most susceptible to infections about seven to ten days from now. She will have a blood test prior to seeing the oncologist. She will have another blood test just before her next chemotherapy infusion in three weeks.

The infusion is making Peg miserable. Infusions affect people differently. After about three hours, so far is so good. In the end, we were at the clinic for eight hours.

Saturday, September 13, 2008

Peg is resting. She has lost all of her hair and she tires easily. From the third day through the eighth day following chemotherapy, Peg developed severe pain in her bones as the toxins attacked her bone marrow. The pain was so intense, oral medicines could not control it. She ended up back at the clinic where she received a Dilaudid shot. Subsequent pain medicine did not reduce the pain more than half way.

Peg is a real trooper. Her will to be a good wife, mother, grandmother, church secretary, and so on has kept her going, together with her strong belief in God and having purpose in life. Our marriage is surely blessed.

Last Tuesday, we met with the oncologist. Although Peg is known to be very sensitive and reactive to chemicals, the oncologist hoped that Peg could make it through chemotherapy without far-reaching adverse reaction. This was not the case.

In agreement with the oncologist, Peg has withdrawn from further chemotherapy. She will be monitored for any cancer recurrence. If it comes back, options will be discussed, including hospitalization to control the pain during chemotherapy and possible radiation. So far so good, and she has begun to go back to work part time.

Wednesday, August 19, 2009

We have lived, loved, and laughed for almost a year since my last entry. Peg is working full time. Her most recent PET scan has shown that she is cancer free. Although, the long term finding will take years to determine, so far is so good. The next scan will take place in March or April, 2010.

One interesting side effect of the aborted chemotherapy is that Peg has curls. She never had curly hair. When her hair grew back, she developed large, stunning curls all over her head. Strangers on the street take a second look when they pass her. They are especially taken aback when she is wearing her t-shirt that reads, "Nope, not a perm."

Addendum

The day after we heard the news from Peg's lung biopsy, I wrote an email to a priest who left our

Episcopal church to take a position in a distant town. I told her our news and that it had been devastating to me. I wrote how Peg wanted me to be strong as a rock for her while I stood by her side. She intended to fight the disease and needed me to be strong.

I continued writing about Peg and how she felt strongly that she had a purpose, specifically, that her presence as church secretary was a calling, much more than a job. Peg had a cadre of staff and volunteers at work who served as a source of encouragement and support.

I wrote about how special Peg is, how good we were together, and that every day, for over twenty years, we have thanked God for bringing us together. Everything I did was for her. I said that we had placed our lives in God's hands and felt that He brought us together for a reason.

I ended by writing about how Peg asked me not to be depressed so that she could fight the disease. I babysat a grandson all day and another before and after school. Then I washed clothes, fixed supper, washed dishes, and interacted with the family. I had no one to talk to or to just sit with and cry. I closed with, "I think that just you knowing how I feel will go a long way." Her thankful response was very kind and compassionate. We still keep in touch.

So, who is my rock? I know at this point in my life that my rock has always been close by my side. God, through Jesus, has been there with me since I can remember. He fully knows my thoughts and my apprehensions. He will be by my side for the rest of my life.

Afterthoughts

After writing the bulk of stories for this book, I began to think about their entirety when viewed together. I had many questions. Why did I have the near-death experience? For the most part, I was not deathly ill. Why didn't I stay and enter the light? Was it because I needed to help Peg through cancer treatments? What was the miracle inherent in the story of meeting the mayor in Malaysia? Why did the mayor ask me if she was all right? Why was the old woman in the woods compelled to tell me those particular words? Does the tenor of the feedback from all that I have influenced have meaning in some way? Why did I document the stories of Ian's encounters with the essence of God?

I have begun to think that the so-called wall between life and death may not be so impervious. We all may be instruments in God's work. Are we building connections on earth? Are we reconstructing Eden? As sinners, are we continually touched by God's never-ending love and forgiveness? And, isn't God for everyone, including First Americans, Malaysians, you, and me, and the rest of us?

How often have you been far from home and told someone where you are from, only to be told, "I was there last week" or, "I used to live there." We respond by murmuring, "Small world." It happens to me all of the time. We love to make associations any way we can. The act comforts us. But, might there be more to it?

How do we come together to be able to make such associations? What are the dynamics? Is it purposeful or random? If purposeful, who is chosen to do what? Are we all moving through life, fulfilling a grand plan?

Whatever we do, it is known that we leave tracks as we pass through life on earth. Some may have a positive impact, some not. You have heard that by means of identifying the right six people, you can connect yourself to every person on earth. I think that this is just a numbers game, but it may reflect a much deeper phenomenon of connectedness, even interdependence.

So, what do we make about my stories of Ian and his talks with Jesus and his guardian angel? What about the old woman in the woods? If the truth were told, are there angels among us? Are they guiding us to each other? Is the threshold between heaven and earth so permeable? Maybe there is more of heaven on earth than we think. Having removed selflessness and hate, maybe we are, or could be in heaven, while we are alive.

One thing that I have learned in this life is that we have today, this moment, to have and to hold.

What counts is what we do with it. We can be givers or takers. We can deposit into or withdraw what life offers us in relationships and natural resources. The more investment, the more return. Yesterday is gone. We cannot depend on putting things off until an unknown tomorrow. We do have tremendous potential to change things for the better, today.

In November 2006, when Ian was six years old, we participated in a talent show at our church retreat. We gave a unique presentation, combining singing (yes, singing) with a solo talk by Ian about how I have affected his life.

I played the keyboard and sang the low notes where I was more or less in tune. I let the keyboard and sound system carry us as I spoke on the high notes. Ian sang all of the melody parts. We worked on Ian's soliloquy together, modifying it until the last moment.

Ian stood on a platform, before a microphone, in front of 150 people. It was very moving, leaving everyone in tears. It focused on the outcome of striving toward a positive impact with each moment of our lives.

The soliloquy was presented during our singing of a slow and meaningful hymn. The presentation reflects on a young boy's gratitude and love for his grandfather. I have reproduced part of Ian's presentation below.

Performance at Shrine Mont Retreat, November 4, 2006
(Ian, Grandson; Nick Brown, Grandfather)

[Ian's Spoken Words]

When did I really get to know you?
Was it when we first went fishing and saw that great
 blue heron standing nearby?
When I thought you wouldn't like me, when I painted
 the sidewalk and you knew I was at fault?
Was it when I first held puppy Dandy or later, when
 you and I ran with him?

Was it when I saw you showing little Austin how to be as good as he can?

Was it when we came down Shrine Mont Mountain and I stopped before the station of the cross where Jesus was nailed to the cross?

You waited for me so very long until I figured it all out.

Remember when we rode so far to see your 104-year old aunt? She said, "I was a good boy."

Later, when you told me she died, it seemed so strange. But, you were there.

Poppa … I love you.

Epilogue

What happened to that twelve year old boy, standing in a walnut grove, making a pact with God? What are the chances of that rural boy becoming the first in the world to get a Ph.D. in Environmental Science? Was it likely that he would teach Ecology to Graduate Students and be behind many of the nation's efforts to purify polluted rivers and lakes, improve the quality of ground water, clean up contaminated lands, and preserve and enhance natural areas?

After sixty years, I think he is still here. He still loves nature. He still wants to please God. He didn't know the real difficulty of staying on the straight and narrow. Ambition, focus on the here-and-now, and lust took their toll. He is much more peaceful now, content, and focused on God's work. He still doesn't know what lies ahead or have much insight into God's plan. But, he knows he is making a difference for the better when he looks into the eyes of Alzheimer patients when bringing communion from church, the eyes of low income elderly when bringing food or needed household goods, the eyes of science fair students when offering encouragement, the eyes of grandchildren when empowering them to do more than take up space, and the eyes of my wife when I say, "forever together" with commitment.

So ... now what? This book is only a part of my journey. I wrote almost all of it from 3:30 a.m. until 8:30 a.m., over a two week period, while overlooking Square Butte and Round Butte on the high plains of northwestern Montana. Babysitting for three grandchildren, daily chores, and focus on Peg's battle with cancer has precluded writing or editing for the last two years. Now, Peg and I are back for another two week vacation.

It is 9:00 p.m. Peg is asleep and the sun will be up for another couple of hours. For me, I have decided to soak up the expanse of landscape, wildlife, and sky, while writing a few reflective thoughts to close this book.

I would like to know what I am going to do with the rest of my life. I suppose doing something profound would be great. But, I know that just doing the day-to-day things with integrity makes a world of difference to others and leaves a legacy far beyond any newfound discovery or notable public accomplishment.

CPSIA information can be obtained
at www.ICGtesting.com
Printed in the USA
FFHW020658060519
52323024-57670FF